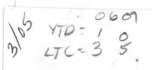

Queen Victoria
and the
British Empire

Queen Victoria and the British Empire

Nancy Whitelaw

**MORGAN
REYNOLDS**
Publishing, Inc.

620 South Elm Street, Suite 223
Greensboro, North Carolina 27406
http://www.morganreynolds.com

European Queens

Queen Isabella
Catherine de' Medici
Catherine the Great
Marie Antoinette
Queen Victoria

QUEEN VICTORIA AND THE BRITISH EMPIRE

Library of Congress Cataloging-in-Publication Data

Whitelaw, Nancy.
Queen Victoria and the British Empire / Nancy Whitelaw.— 1st ed.
   p. cm. — (European queens)
Includes bibliographical references and index.
ISBN 1-931798-29-X (lib. bdg.)
1. Victoria, Queen of Great Britain, 1819-1901—Juvenile literature. 2. Great
Britain—Colonies—Administration—History—19th century—Juvenile literature. 3.
Great Britain—History—Victoria, 1837-1901—Juvenile literature. 4. Queens—Great
Britain—Biography—Juvenile literature. I. Title. II. World leaders (Greensboro,
N.C.)
   DA557.W46 2004
   941.081'092—dc22

                       2004008410

Printed in the United States of America
First Edition

To Kristen Wright
with love and thanks for all your help

Contents

1

The New Queen

Early on the morning of June 20, 1837, the seventy-two-year-old king of Great Britain was pronounced dead. William IV had been ill for some time; his death was not unexpected. Only a few hours after William's last breath, his doctor, along with the Archbishop of Canterbury and a few other government officials, climbed into a carriage and hurried to Kensington Palace, twenty miles away. The delegation arrived just after six in the morning, demanded entry, and told the sleepy servant who opened the door to awaken Princess Victoria immediately.

A few minutes later, eighteen-year-old Victoria stood nervously before them. Dawn was breaking over London when, in accordance with tradition, the Archbishop of Canterbury solemnly informed Victoria that she was now

Opposite: Queen Victoria with her two eldest children, Vicky and Bertie.

Princess Victoria being informed of the death of William IV. *(Courtesy of Art Resource.)*

the queen of England. The purpose of their visit completed, the functionaries made their retreat and left the young queen alone.

Victoria had planned for this day and knew what to do. She sent for Lord Melbourne, who was both the prime minister and her closest advisor in government. She had grown fond of Melbourne and trusted his advice and, most importantly, his motives. She was convinced he loved England as much as she did. After sending for the prime minister, she withdrew to her rooms and spent a few minutes recording her thoughts in her journal, a lifelong habit. "I am very young and . . . inexperienced," she wrote, "but I am sure that very few have more real good will and more real desire to do what is fit and right than I have."

Less than six hours after learning of William's death, Victoria held her first cabinet meeting in a room in Kensington Palace called the Red Salon. Dressed in mourning clothes, she was a tiny figure, not quite five feet tall, and still quite slim. She bowed to the assembly, then read aloud, in a firm and decisive voice, her declaration to accept the crown and to work always for the good of the people of Great Britain. At no time did she display any emotion or hesitation or seem overwhelmed by the immense responsibility placed on her young shoulders. The members of the cabinet were impressed by her poise, self-confidence, and obvious intelligence—a refreshing change from the royals who had preceded her.

Victoria holds her first council as queen of England. Even though she is in mourning, she is depicted here in white to contrast against all the men in the room.

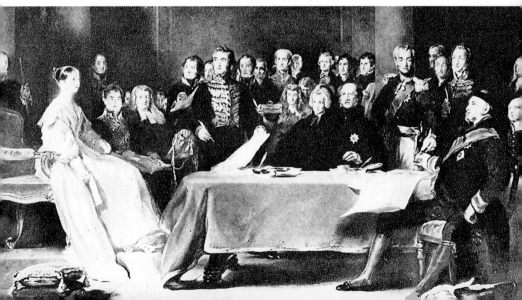

Immediately after her first meeting with her council, Victoria said to her mother, the Duchess of Kent, "Let me be by myself for an hour." She had suffered for years under her mother's tight control. Now she was free. She had her bed moved out of her mother's room and into separate quarters. The duchess was not allowed to attend conferences with the privy council or the queen's discussions with Melbourne. At her first opportunity, Victoria removed her mother's confidante, John Conroy, from the court. She knew John Conroy wanted her power for himself. She gave him a token reward for his services and had him sent away. Victoria's mother was furious at Conroy's dismissal and wrote angrily to her daughter, "You do not know the world." The duchess may have been right, but Victoria was determined that she would learn about it on her own terms.

The throne Victoria inherited sat atop an enormous empire that encompassed Scotland, Wales, Ireland, and the continent of Australia; much of modern-day Canada, India, and Pakistan; and colonies in Africa and Malaysia, in addition to several islands around the world. England had once claimed possession of most of the eastern seaboard of North America, and the loss of the thirteen colonies that later joined together to form the United States was still felt bitterly, particularly among the royalty and the wealthy who had once profited from the bountiful natural resources of the New World. Losing the American colonies had made the British holdings in India that much more important—India also had substantial natural resources.

Holding the entire vast empire together was difficult and

A world map showing British colonial possessions in 1837. *(Courtesy of Getty Images.)*

expensive. Some territories, like the colonies in America and the island of Ireland, resisted British occupation more than others. Britain developed and maintained a large navy, which helped the small island nation (smaller than the American state of Oregon) reap the benefits of and police its colonies abroad. British possessions, combined with the wealth created by the newly developing Industrial Revolution, had, by Victoria's ascension in 1837, made Great Britain the richest and most powerful country in the world.

But rapid growth had also created many problems. British industrial development was accompanied by a huge increase in population—from nine million to fourteen million people in just over fifty years. People were leaving the countryside and migrating to cities in search of work. Once there, families lived crammed into unsanitary tenement houses. There were no sewer systems, which made the water extremely unsafe—outbreaks of cholera, dysentery, and typhoid were common throughout the nineteenth century. Working conditions were also hazardous. In some cities, the life expectancy of an average worker was only seventeen years.

The Industrial Revolution created new wealth, which was accumulated by the growing middle class. The landed aristocracy, a small group of old families, had traditionally governed Britain. But the growing middle class had money

A tosher, or sewage scavenger, in early nineteenth-century London.

and paid taxes and began to demand power and influence—demands backed by their formidable financial power. Workers, too, began to advocate for better working and living conditions, higher wages, and better public services. Trade unions began to form early in the century. The nineteenth century in Great Britain, and elsewhere, was dominated by domestic issues.

The great political battles of the era concerned questions of governmental reform: who should be allowed to vote; how the representative districts, or boroughs, were to be determined; how high taxes should be and who should pay them; and sundry similar issues. Four years before Victoria was born, the country had been wracked by conflict over the infamous Corn Law of 1815. Its intention was to protect British landowners, mostly the aristocracy, from having to compete with foreign-grown wheat by imposing high tariffs on imports. Because the supply of wheat was so limited, prices became extremely high. Bread and other staple goods were prohibitively expensive. Thousands took to the streets at rallies, demanding a repeal of the Corn Laws. It would take decades for this to happen.

Amid domestic discord, Victoria's biggest challenge throughout her reign would be determining her proper constitutional role in the highly complicated British political system. Beginning with the Magna Carta in 1215, through the civil war of the seventeenth century (during which one king had lost his head), and the Glorious Revolution of 1688 (during which another king lost his job), there was ongoing tension and conflict between the crown and the elected Parliament. Officially, Victoria had impressive power. She could collapse a government by dismissing the cabinet. She could appoint court and other governmental officials, and, most importantly, she could dissolve Parliament and call for new elections. But in reality, the monarch's power was severely limited. The real power was with the elected Parliament and the prime minister—the leader of the party that held the most seats in the House of Commons. The queen needed to be consulted and to officially sign off on many decisions, and to publicly support the government, but the process of history had, by the nineteenth century, successfully turned the British monarchy into a largely ceremonial post.

But being queen was important, nonetheless. She could do much good—or ill. The story of her Hanoverian ancestors did not make most British citizens proud. Even before that early summer morning when she became the eighteen-year-old queen of England, Victoria had determined this would change. Years before, at age eleven, when she first learned that it was probable she would one day become queen, she had vowed to "be good" when that responsibility fell on her shoulders.

2

An Uncertain Childhood

Victoria's very birth had been the result of a series of political calculations. In November 1817, Princess Charlotte, the future King George IV's twenty-one-year-old daughter and heir apparent to the British throne, died unexpectedly, while giving birth to a stillborn child. Charlotte was married to a German prince, Leopold of Saxe-Coburg, who would later become both Victoria's uncle and the king of Belgium.

The death of Charlotte and her baby left the ruling family in a precarious position. King George III was old and considered insane. While thirteen of his fifteen children were still alive, they were all well into middle age or beyond. The prince regent, also named George, despised his father and was almost equally despised by his father's subjects. Charlotte had been his only legitimate child. His five sisters

Edward, Duke of Kent.

had no children. Two of his brothers were married, but none had produced an heir.

One of the king's sons, Edward, Duke of Kent, who was fifty when Charlotte died, had lived for years with his mistress. However, he was always short of money and realized that if he married and produced an heir, he would be granted a healthy allowance for the future monarch's upkeep. The recently widowed Leopold of Saxe-Coburg suggested that his sister, herself a widow and the mother of two daughters, would make a suitable bride. Edward, Duke of Kent, and Princess Victoire of Leiningen, who was twenty years younger than her new husband, were married on July 11, 1818. Edward's brother William, Duke of Clarence, who would later become William IV, was also quickly married.

Normally, royal marriages were occasions for celebration. However, because Edward's marriage was so obviously the consequence of naked political ambition and financial calculation, and because the royal family had been such a drain on the nation's treasury for decades, Edward and Victoire were married in a simple ceremony. Soon after their wedding, they were forced by poverty to return to Victoire's home of Saxe-Coburg, a small state in what is now Germany. Victoire soon discovered that Edward was financially irresponsible and that the newlyweds were deeply in debt.

Happily, Victoire was soon able to inform her husband that she was pregnant. Edward was thrilled, and immediately began scheming to get the money to ensure that his child would be born on British soil. After months of begging and maneuvering, Edward, his pregnant wife, and eleven carriages of servants, household goods, and pets arrived in England. Two months later, on May 24, 1819, Victoire delivered a healthy baby girl. When Edward heard the news, he said, "Take care of her, for she will one day be Queen of England."

Edward had no way of knowing if his assertion would become true. For most of her youth, Victoria was not the heir apparent. Her uncle William, the future William IV, was an old man, but his wife was much younger, so there was always the possibility she would have a child. In fact, she had so many uncles that, at her birth, Victoria was only fifth in line to the throne. The prince regent, the future George IV, who disliked his brother Edward and his new wife, and was still upset over the death of his daughter, even refused to allow the baby to be christened with any of the names traditionally reserved for female members of the royal family. He insisted that she be called Alexandrina in honor of her godfather, Czar Alexander I of Russia, who had been chosen for political purposes. He then grudgingly admitted that if she had to have a second name (and almost every royal had at least two), she could share her mother's name of Victoria.

George thought his brother Edward was greedy, careless, and a drain on his time, energy, and finances. He urged Edward to take his wife and newly baptized daughter back to Saxe-Coburg, but Edward wanted to keep Victoria close to the throne. Though he had little money, he managed to find the family a small cottage in the country. They had hardly settled in when Edward contracted pneumonia. Although doctors hovered over him, bleeding him repeatedly

by applying leeches to his skin, Edward died. He left behind an eight-month-old daughter and a now twice-widowed wife who spoke almost no English and had few friends.

But the Duchess of Kent did have one asset. She was the mother of a child who might someday be queen. The duchess looked to her

Victoire, the Duchess of Kent.

brother Leopold for help. Leopold, who still lived in England, was not popular with the British. Parliament had granted him a handsome annuity when he married Charlotte that could not be rescinded now that Charlotte was dead. It was a constant source of irritation to many people that this handsome young German prince was enjoying a luxurious lifestyle—which included a German mistress—funded by the British public treasury. As he became involved in Victoria's upbringing many whispered that the foreigner Leopold was bitter at having been denied the British throne by his wife's death, and now sought to regain it through his niece.

Leopold, a savvy political operator, heard all the rumors and realized they could damage his own hopes for advancement. He needed to distance himself from his sister and

This cartoon from 1830, entitled "Design for a Regency," shows Leopold entertaining Princess Victoria on his knee while the duchess sits on the throne and Sir John Conroy presides over an imaginary meeting of the privy council.

niece. He gave the duchess some money; not much, but more than the British government would provide. He also negotiated with George IV to allow the duchess and her baby daughter to live in Kensington Palace, where Victoria had been born. After that, he mostly stayed away.

Victoire began to turn to Captain John Conroy, who had promised the dying Duke of Kent to watch after his wife and child, for help and advice. Conroy, who had been one of Edward's closest friends, was a handsome Irishman exactly the duchess's age. It soon became apparent, however, that the duke's trust in his old friend had been misplaced. Conroy was a greedy man who dreamed of having access to the vast royal fortune. He took advantage of the duchess's trusting nature. Both George IV and his brother William were old and in poor health. If Victoria inherited the throne before she was eighteen, a regent would have to be appointed. If Conroy could maintain psychological control over the duchess, and she was named as regent, then he would be the real power behind the throne. It was possible that, even after Victoria was of age, he could, with the help of the duchess, continue to manipulate her.

Conroy set out to isolate the duchess and her daughter from the court. One part of his scheme was to convince the German-born duchess, who always felt out of place in England, that everyone at court was against her. The fact that both of her brothers-in-law did not like her made his job easier. Conroy even hinted that the uncles might plot to kill Victoria.

Under pressure from Conroy, Victoria was raised in near-complete isolation. Her early childhood was lonely and sheltered. One of her few companions was her half-sister, Feodora. She was also allowed to play with Conroy's daughter, whom she disliked. But most of her time was spent in the company of her devoted nanny and tutor, Louise Lehzen. Lehzen, the daughter of a German clergyman, had been brought to England

Princess Victoria as a young child.

to care for the little girl. The Duchess of Kent refused to entrust Victoria to British hands. Lehzen, Conroy, and the duchess kept a close watch over young Victoria—she was not even allowed to go up or down stairs without someone they trusted there to hold her hand.

It was a suffocating childhood, but Victoria proved willing, from an early age, to fight for some distance from the controlling adults. Her temper tantrums became notorious. Generally, she was an adorable child, with a sunny disposition and a capacity for compassion and understanding that was remarkable in one so young. But she would often fly into rages, sometimes with little provocation, then come back to her gentle self just as quickly. Once, her mother reported to a tutor that Victoria had thrown a tantrum the day before. But the four-year-old Victoria corrected her: "Two storms," she said, "one at dressing, and one at washing." When the duchess tried to appeal to her daughter's better nature by saying that her temper made them both unhappy, Victoria was unconvinced: "No, Mama," she replied, "not *me*, not myself, but *you*." Even Victoria's piano teacher was not spared the princess's fury. Having just told her young charge she must practice if she wanted to improve, the teacher was startled when the little girl slammed the piano lid shut and declared: "There, now! You see there is no *must* about it at all."

Although she did not learn how likely it was that she would become queen until she was older, Victoria was a perceptive child who noticed how people acted around her early on. When she and her half-sister Feodora went riding in the park, men tipped their hats only to her. Though she did not fully understand what this meant, she soon grew to expect deference from others.

Louise Lehzen was the most skillful at controlling Victoria's imperious manner. She insisted that her young charge apologize for any bad behavior. She also insisted on good manners. Victoria received a private education, although she was not a scholar. She had lessons in history, geography, Latin, religion, handwriting, English poetry, music, dancing, French, German, and sketching. To encourage a regal bearing, she was often required to wear a spring of holly pinned to her collar. If she forgot to hold her head up, the sharp points of the holly reminded her. A lonely child because of the fears and schemes of her mother and Conroy, her closest companions were dolls. She had over one hundred, and spent a great deal of time designing elaborate costumes and houses for them. It was a quiet childhood, and

King William IV.

though she was often sad, Victoria later said it had been "a great blessing and advantage to have lived in such simple and restricted circumstances."

In 1830, King George IV died. Now Uncle Willie, who was sixty-five, became King William IV. William had no living children. Although his wife, whom he had married in the same rush that brought Victoria's parents together, was still of childbearing age, the next in line to the throne was now an eleven-year-old girl.

It was time for Victoria to learn her destiny. Louise Lehzen had long ago been instructed to remove a page from one of Victoria's books diagramming the royal succession—Victoria's family tree. Now she was told to slip it back in. When the young princess found the page, she studied it closely, then remarked calmly, "I see I am nearer the throne than I

Princess Victoria with her mother.

thought." Legend has it that she then held up one finger, which was a characteristic mannerism, and said: "I will be good."

Now that Victoria's acscension seemed all but inevitable, the duchess and Conroy lobbied to have the duchess appointed regent. This was the culmination of their plans. But William distrusted Conroy's motives and managed to have the regency appointment squashed.

Despite this setback, the duchess grew more confident. She enjoyed flaunting her new role. She became a popular society hostess. No one could refuse an invitation from the mother of the future queen. At the end of these elaborate parties the princess was produced momentarily for the company's admiration.

On her fourteenth birthday, Princess Victoria greeted her

diary with the words "I am today fourteen years old! How very old!" Her Uncle Leopold, now the king of Belgium, sent a cautionary message: "You are now fourteen years old, a period when the delightful pastimes of childhood must be mixed with thoughts appertaining already to a matured part of your life." He told her to trust her own common sense and her idea of truth, and that the business of the state was "to act with great impartiality and a spirit of justice for the good of all." Victoria appreciated his concern and told her journal, "I look up to him [Leopold] as a Father, with complete confidence, love and affection."

Leopold had long kept an eye on Victoria from a distance. He did not trust Conroy and knew the duchess was under his influence. Now that Victoria was nearing the age of independence, eighteen, Leopold sent one of his close advisors to England to assess the situation. Baron Christian

Sir John Conroy.

Stockmar quickly realized the negative influence John Conroy had over the duchess. He wrote to his brother that the princess was suffering under their controlling hands. Leopold wanted to intervene, but knew any move he made would give rise to gossip that he had designs on the British throne. But he had recently married and decided to use this as an excuse to visit England to show off his young bride.

Leopold's visit thrilled Victoria. She was finally allowed to attend dinners, instead of being kept in the wings and presented for only a few minutes before dessert. She met the new queen of Belgium and was captivated by her beauty and fashionable clothes. Leopold had married a Catholic in order to appease the mostly Catholic population of Belgium. Victoria had been raised in accordance with the Church of England and trained to believe Catholicism was objectionable. But Leopold's sweet and beautiful wife contradicted what Victoria had been told. From this time on she became stronger in her commitment to religious freedom. Every person, Victoria believed, should be free to worship as he or she chose.

Soon after Leopold left, Victoria became very ill. The fever was probably typhoid. She was in bed for almost five weeks. During this dangerous time, Conroy tried to use her weakness to his advantage by asking her to sign a pledge to make him her private secretary when she became queen. Although terribly sick, Victoria refused, even when her mother joined Conroy in pressuring her. She later wrote proudly to her Uncle Leopold, "I resisted in spite of my illness." Undeterred, Conroy spread rumors that Victoria was frail and implied that her poor health would make her a weak queen.

When Victoria finally left her sickbed, it was to find a parade of suitors outside her door. Though she was not yet queen, people were already jockeying to influence her. Leopold wanted her to marry into his side of the family, someone from Saxe-Coburg, such as her first cousin Albert. King William wanted her to marry a relative from the British side. For her part, Victoria was not interested in marrying anyone. She knew any marriage she made would be a political alliance. She chafed at the idea of finally being free of her controlling mother only to surrender herself to a husband. As her eighteenth birthday neared, Victoria was focused on one thing: preparing herself to become queen. Her Uncle William was elderly and ill.

On her eighteenth birthday, Victoria wrote in her diary, "How far I am from being what I should be. I shall from this day take the firm resolution to study with renewed assiduity . . . and to strive to become every day less trifling and more fit for what, if Heaven wills it, I'm some day to be."

The two people who provided Victoria with the support she needed to develop her independence of mind and, someday, to stand up to her mother and Conroy, were Louise Lehzen and Leopold. Lehzen told Victoria repeatedly to trust herself. Leopold, more practically, told her to contact Lord Melbourne as soon as King William died.

Coronation

On August 20, 1836, the night before King William's seventieth birthday, Victoria, the duchess, and a hundred other guests gathered for a celebratory dinner at Windsor Castle. In response to a toast, the old king praised Victoria and told her how happy he was that she was there. He said pointedly, "I hope royal authority will turn" to Victoria, and not to "the person now near me, who is surrounded by evil advisors." The shocked guests realized immediately the king was referring to the duchess and her "evil advisor" Conroy.

The king managed to keep the duchess and Conroy away from the throne by living for nine more months, until Victoria was of legal age and would not need a regent.

So it was that on the morning of June 20, 1837, after receiving news of William's death, the new queen remembered the advice she had been given. Ignoring her mother and Conroy, she took her first steps alone and called upon the services of Lord Melbourne, the leader of the Whig Party.

Melbourne was a fifty-eight year old widower who was still grieving over the recent death of his only son. A handsome man, rumored to be on close terms with some of the ladies of the court, Melbourne devoted most of his time and energy to politics and to his country. Although he had dabbled in radical politics as a young man, age and experience had made him

Lord Melbourne.

more conservative. Melbourne had been prime minister twice before; Victoria could not have found a better or more devoted advisor.

Victoria confessed to Melbourne that she knew very little about politics but was willing to learn. Melbourne established what was essentially a tutor-student relationship with the young queen. Victoria learned about the recent political

A mid-nineteenth-century view of British Parliament from the river Thames. *(Courtesy of Art Resource.)*

history of England, who the important people of the age were, and about the peculiar customs of the British aristocracy and government.

Victoria learned from Melbourne that some of the previous kings and queens of England preferred to play major roles in government, while others were content to be figureheads. She studied the Parliament, which had two houses— the House of Lords, made up of hereditary and appointed members, and the House of Commons, which consisted of elected representatives. Members of Parliament, who were responsible for introducing and voting on bills, were also members of political parties. The party that won the most votes in each election controlled the government. The prime minister, who was also a member of Parliament, was the leader of the majority party. He was officially "invited" to form a government by the reigning monarch. The prime minister appointed about one hundred ministers, of which about twenty made up his cabinet. The party out of power organized a "shadow" government, which kept close tabs on those in office. The government could fall at any time. For example, the defeat of an important bill that was supported by the government often motivated the opposition party to call for a vote of "no confidence." If that vote succeeded, the government would be collapsed and a new prime minister appointed.

There were two major political parties during Victoria's time: the Whigs, who generally represented the middle class and those whose wealth came from business, and the Tories, the more conservative party, supported primarily by the landed aristocracy. There was no viable party representing the interests of workers and the urban poor, mainly because they could not vote. The Whigs favored a certain level of governmental reforms, free trade over tariffs, and the expansion of the empire. The Tories tended to favor restrictions on trade, less reform, and the maintaining of class distinctions.

The French Revolution, which began in 1789, had terrified the aristocracy of England. The people of France had risen up to overthrow the ruling monarchy and to establish a republic that rejected the idea of a class system. Over the next quarter century the French king and queen, along with a sizable number of aristocrats, had been executed in a bloody purge that culminated in the reign of Napoleon Bonaparte, a former artillery officer. Napoleon declared himself emperor and began an aggressive campaign to gain more territory that ended with his famous defeat at Waterloo in 1815. Fearful that what happened to France could happen elsewhere, most European nations installed conservative governments determined to avoid similar revolutions.

Monarchies across Europe were horrified when King Louis XVI of France and many members of his family were executed by guillotine during the French Revolution.

The British ruling class, too, was determined to quash any movements for political or economic reform. At first, they succeeded at keeping a tight lid on the country. But by the early to mid-1830s, the social and economic conditions created by the Industrial Revolution brought on more and more demands for reform.

The landed aristocracy still controlled the machinery of British politics. But they were challenged more and more often by the increasingly wealthy middle class, as well as by the large number of urban workers and the poor. The middle class and the urban workers bore the brunt of the tax burden. Any attempt to fix this ran into the political reality of the so-called rotten boroughs. These were districts that had as few as twenty voters but were still allowed to send a representative to Parliament. Invariably, the eligible voters were under the control of a powerful family who could hand-select a candidate to watch out for their interests. There was no process of redistricting, so these problems had festered for years. Socially and politically, when Victoria became queen, Britain was a powder keg.

Although Victoria initially knew little about party politics, she knew her father had been a Whig and that she planned to follow in his footsteps. She said publicly that she detested Tories as much as she detested insects and turtle soup. This was a foolish and rash statement. The monarchy was expected to be as apolitical as possible. By aligning herself with the Whigs, Victoria was only setting herself up for trouble when the Tories came to power.

Victoria was the first female ruler of England since the death of Queen Anne in 1714. The early months of her reign were a whirlwind of fittings, meetings, and conferences. She was schooled in the protocol of everything from properly addressing ambassadors to negotiating with the heads of other countries. Some of her duties included the ceremonial inspection of troops, which she found thrilling. She sat proudly on her horse as the gleaming ranks of soldiers marched by. She confided in her journal: "I felt for the first time like a man, as if I could fight myself at the head of my Troops."

Though her mother had tried to isolate her, young Victoria had been sent on several quick tours of England. Her mother had given her a small leather notebook in which to record her observations of each day's travel, and she would continue that ritual for the rest of her life.

Victoria's first trips were also her introduction to poverty.

Victoria is pictured here on horseback, flanked by her advisors.

One journal entry shows the pain she felt upon seeing the desperate mining towns of Wales: "The Country continues black, engines flaming, coals, in abundance, everywhere, smoking and burning coal heaps, intermingled with wretched huts and carts and little ragged children."

The Industrial Revolution needed hundreds of thousands of workers to fuel its mines and machines, and many of those workers were children—some as young as three years old. As teenage Victoria was touring England, reform committees were petitioning the government to pass laws restricting child labor. The Reform Act of 1832, which would make political representation in Parliament more equitable by extending the right to vote and reforming electoral districts, galvanized the reform movement. In 1833, Parliament voted that children over the age of eleven could not work more than twelve hours a day, those between nine and eleven no more than eight hours a day, and children under nine could not legally work at all. But these new restrictions applied only to the textile industry. Children who worked in mines, other kinds of factories, or various construction-related fields could still be forced to put in twelve, fourteen, or even sixteen hours a day. Few had any schooling; many died young. In 1847, Parliament would finally pass a law limiting all people to a maximum ten-hour workday. Still, dangerous conditions and low pay were the norm.

A popular novel of the day was Charles Dickens's *Oliver Twist,* which first appeared in 1837, the year Victoria became queen. Dickens was a proponent of social reform. He used his novels to portray and decry the miserable conditions of the working class in England. Victoria read *Oliver Twist* and was startled by the world Dickens described. When she tried to speak to Melbourne about it he first avoided her questions, then finally said bluntly, "I don't *like* those things." Melbourne told Victoria the purpose of government was to prevent and punish crime and preserve contracts, not to care for those who could not care for

This nineteenth-century engraving shows children in a workhouse lining up on payday.

themselves. His final words on the subject were "Why bother with the poor? Leave them alone."

Melbourne's attitude was not unusual. The Industrial Revolution was enriching and empowering a growing middle class, who did not want the government to restrict how they accumulated wealth. The landed aristocracy was still in control of politics, even after the Reform Bill. The poor, who were not allowed to vote, were further disenfranchised by the Poor Law of 1834. This law reflected the popular assumption of the middle and upper classes that people were poor only because they did not work hard enough. The Poor Law was designed to offer them a chance to earn their way out of poverty through the establishment of workhouses, the very things Dickens reviled in his novels based on his first-hand knowledge, having worked in one until he was ten years old.

These workhouses provided jobs and food to those who had neither, but were designed to pay less than the worst-paying job available and to create living conditions more miserable than the most degraded slum. The theory was that if people were faced with such intolerable conditions, they would be more likely to want to find their own jobs. The problem with this idea was that not everyone was capable of finding better jobs—the elderly, the very young, the sick, and the mentally infirm all languished in these miserable conditions and in other types of public charity.

Outside of the workhouses, conditions were not much better. Children were still forced to labor for ten or twelve hours a day, and there were no laws to ensure clean water or to enforce other sanitary measures. Disease was common, public executions were popular events, and widespread poverty and starvation made death a constant presence in most people's lives. Very little was done during Victoria's reign for those who needed help most. In her defense, it is true that Victoria knew little about the privations of her people. She was protected from their plight by everyone around her. She also had little actual power to make changes in public policy.

Each morning, Victoria was kept busy reading, writing letters, and transacting state business with Melbourne. She never complained about her workload, writing in her journal: "I received so many communications from my Ministers, but I like it very much . . . I *delight* in this work." In the afternoons, she usually went riding, after which she played a game or listened to music. Evenings were formal occasions, constrained by strict rules of etiquette. Guests were seated but unable to eat until Victoria came into the room, sometimes thirty or forty minutes later. She was always served first, and everyone's plates were removed as soon as the queen was done with her meal. Victoria's appetite was soon legendary, and the smart guest learned to eat fast if he were going to dine at her table. One member of her court said of her: "she laughs in real earnest, opening her mouth as wide as it can go . . . she eats quite as heartily as she laughs. I think I may say she gobbles."

After dinner, Victoria would make the rounds of her guests, asking each one a simple question such as "Did you enjoy riding today?" The guest would quickly respond, "Oh, yes, your majesty," and she would move on. No one else was allowed to talk during this circuit. Once the visiting was over, the diners would adjourn to another room to play cards or chess or listen to piano or voice recitals. The queen loved dancing and parties, often staying at balls until dawn. Before she could begin to dance, the queen would be presented with any number of people, each of whom would file past her seat, be introduced, bow or curtsey, and kiss her hand. Some nights, those presented numbered well into the thousands.

During her early reign, Victoria was grateful to have the advice and council of Lord Melbourne. Soon after their first meeting, her journal began filling up with admiring comments about the man she called "Lord M." He was a great help to her as she navigated unfamiliar and dangerous political shores. Still, Victoria's independent spirit shone through. Once, Melbourne told her she was scheduled to review her troops while riding in a carriage. Victoria balked, saying she wanted to be on horseback for the ceremony. Melbourne refused her request, and she said simply, "Very well, my lord, very well—remember, no horse, no review." Melbourne would not give in, and the review was cancelled.

Victoria began to assert herself in other ways. She shut her mother almost completely out of her life, and relied only on Lehzen, Melbourne, and Stockmar for advice. They did their best to restrain the headstrong young queen. Part of Victoria's coronation ceremony required her to swear to uphold "the Protestant reformed religion," the official religion of England. But the first person she knighted was an old friend and neighbor, who was Jewish. One of her most strongly held beliefs was that religion was a personal matter.

In the fall of 1837, Victoria described the past months as being the most pleasant summer she could remember. Her confidence was growing every day and she enjoyed her new responsibilities—though not everything she had to do was easy. Her Uncle Leopold had been her staunch supporter for years. She was very grateful for his advice and help, but her instinct said she could not repay his kindness to her with state favors. Leopold wrote to her to ask that she influence her court to support Belgium in a diplomatic quarrel with France and Holland. Victoria replied by asking him not to petition her for political favors. When he pressed the matter, she held firm: "Upon this one subject we cannot agree. I shall, therefore, limit myself to my expressions of very sincere wishes for the welfare and prosperity of Belgium."

Though Victoria was considered to be queen from the

moment of William's last breath, she was not officially crowned until June 28, 1838, almost a year later. Her coronation was a lavish event; designed for the sole purpose of showing the land that while the queen might not rule the country, she was still the symbolic representative of God on earth. Melbourne took charge of the ceremony, which began with the symbolic firing of canons at four o'clock in the morning. Victoria and most of London were up early.

At ten, Victoria's procession set out for Westminster Abbey, the great Gothic cathedral in which every coronation since 1066 had been held. Victoria's carriage took a circuitous route to allow as many people as possible to catch a glimpse. Nearly 400,000 people lined the streets. Victoria rode for an hour and a half, carrying the orb and scepter, a jeweled globe that represented the queen's position as the head of the Church of England, and a decorated staff with a cross, which represented the queen's power under the cross. As she approached Westminster Abbey, an orchestra announced her arrival with a tremendous crash of music.

Inside, Victoria was dressed in a red velvet robe trimmed with ermine and gold lace and fastened by a golden cord. Her tiny frame seemed even smaller beneath the heavy coronation robe as she proceeded slowly down the center aisle, followed by eight trainbearers. Westminster Abbey was hung with gold and crimson awnings and the floors were covered with Oriental carpets. During the five-hour ceremony, Victoria swore to preserve the Church of England and to protect the country from all harm both from within and without its borders.

Queen Victoria in her coronation robes.

Though the ceremony was serious, even solemn, there were some mishaps. Victoria had not been adequately prepared for the ritual and several times had to whisper questions to the clergy. The bishops accidentally started the litany before she was crowned, and the archbishop squeezed the coronation ring onto Victoria's fourth finger, though it had been fitted for her fifth. Finally, as the service came to a close, the archbishop ceremonially anointed Victoria then placed on her head the splendid crown dazzling with diamonds, pearls, rubies, and a huge sapphire. At that moment, a signal was given and all across London guns were fired, drums played, trumpets sounded, and people shouted "God save the queen!"

Almost nine hours after she had left for the ceremony, Victoria returned to the palace, once again tracing a slow path through the cheering crowds. That evening, she attended a state banquet before watching fireworks in her honor. She told her journal that the crowds' "good humor and excessive loyalty was beyond everything, and I really cannot say how proud I feel to be the Queen of *such* a Nation."

Queen Victoria was immediately popular. Her court and

Victoria's coronation ceremony at Westminster Abbey. *(Courtesy of Getty Images.)*

subjects saw her as a virtuous young lady, a refreshing change from those who preceded her—the mentally un- stable George III, George IV the womanizer, and William IV who had ten illegitimate children. There had been an entire generation of princes, including Victoria's father, who were remembered mostly for their private vices and bad tempers. Victoria seemed to have none of these faults. She had a regal bearing, a responsive look, and large blue eyes. Those who wanted to detract from her generally focused on her physical appearance by saying she was homely, with a too-wide mouth that showed her gums when she laughed.

Though she started out popular, Victoria's habit of mak- ing hasty judgments soon lost her some of the goodwill of her people. One day, after she had banished her mother's consort, John Conroy, from court, she saw him getting into a carriage with one of the court's unmarried ladies-in- waiting, Lady Flora Hastings. A few weeks after this event, Victoria and the rest of the court noticed that Lady Flora appeared to be pregnant. Victoria was quick to assume John Conroy was the father. Rumors began to circulate. Victoria had never liked Lady Flora and seized the opportunity to condemn both her and Conroy.

The queen's participation in the scandalmongering had a galvanizing effect. The press leaped into the fray; Lady Flora's virtue was the subject of much public discussion. Members of the court quickly took sides, most of them agreeing with the queen. Lady Flora's supporters denied the accusations, but their claims fell on deaf ears as Lady Flora's midsection continued to grow. Finally, Victoria ordered

Lady Flora to undergo a doctor's examination to prove she was telling the truth. It was an unprecedented command, given that doctors at the time almost never saw their female patients any way but fully clothed, but Lady Flora submitted to it. When the doctor reported to Victoria that Lady Flora was not pregnant, Victoria apologized to her privately but made no public statement. Six months after the rumors had begun, Lady Flora died of liver cancer—the swelling had been a tumor.

When the full story emerged, public opinion turned against queen. Some people even blamed her for Lady Flora's death. When Victoria went out in public, crowds hissed. In official ceremonies, some gentlemen refused to raise their hats, and many refused to take part in the customary toasts to the queen. A few months later, a man eventually judged a lunatic attempted to kill her. Whether or not he was motivated to do so by Lady Flora's death is unknown; but his actions created an earnest, if brief, wave of public good feel-ing toward the queen.

Victoria's next public relations di-saster was a result of inexperience. When she was crowned queen, she had so few acquaintances outside of her own home that she was

Lady Flora Hastings.

unable to choose the members of her court. Melbourne stepped in to help, but foolishly named a court made up almost entirely of Whigs or their wives. When Melbourne's government failed, in 1839, the Tories came to power. Victoria grudgingly had to appoint a new prime minister— this time, Sir Robert Peel. Peel was well known for his organization of the London metropolitan police force. They were called "bobbies," a play on his first name, as an expression of gratitude.

Peel's ministry was derailed by what came to be known as the Bedchamber Crisis. When he took office, Peel set about, as was customary, replacing Whigs with Tories at all levels of government. It had not escaped his attention that Victoria's bedchamber ladies were all Whigs. He asked her to consider replacing some of her ladies with the wives of Tories. Victoria was indignant at his request—she considered these women personal attendants, not political appointees. A wiser, more experienced queen might have recognized this small sacrifice would earn her a better working relationship with the prime minister. Victoria did not wish to compromise.

Peel stated that he would not take office unless Victoria surrendered some of her attendants. Victoria made it clear she would not. Peel had no choice but to resign and Melbourne's government was returned to power. Victoria would soon enough have reason to regret her stubbornness.

4

A Royal Wedding

Young Queen Victoria, monarch of the most powerful country in the world, was naturally the center of a great deal of matrimonial speculation and maneuvering. She did not see herself as a prize, but as a woman who should make her own decisions about whom she married. She insisted that she would not be rushed into marriage. She was not interested in being anyone's wife, and declared that "it was 10 to 1 that I shouldn't agree with anybody." Victoria intended to be a powerful queen, and simply could not see the need for a husband.

King Leopold, Victoria's royal uncle, believed that the queen was in great need of a husband. To Leopold, marriages were not about love or partnership or even happiness. Where royals were concerned, marriages were about political necessity. Watching from Belgium, Leopold thought

Victoria needed the influence of a calming hand—and he knew just who that calming hand should be. He and his old confidant Baron Stockmar set about bringing together Victoria and Leopold's nephew Albert.

Albert was Victoria's first cousin. The Duchess of Kent was his aunt, his father's sister. The royal families of Europe had a long tradition of intermarriage. It was a way of making and strengthening alliances, but it also had a practical purpose: royalty had to make marriages that befitted their status. There were no options outside other royal families. And since there was no taboo about cousins marrying, many royals were married within their own families.

Prince Albert of Saxe-Coburg and Queen Victoria had met a few times as children but did not know each other well. In October of 1839, Leopold and Stockmar brought Albert and his brother to London. Victoria and her court welcomed their royal guests with a lavish dinner, after which there was dancing. Victoria and Albert were allowed to dance together, but only in certain styles—the newly popular waltz, which would have required Albert to hold Victoria around the waist, was forbidden. The young couple sat and talked and Albert played the piano. That night, the nineteen-year-old queen wrote in her journal "Albert really is quite charming, and so excessively handsome." In another entry, she added that he "has a beautiful nose and a very sweet mouth with fine teeth; but the charm of his countenance is his expression, which is most delightful . . . full of goodness and sweetness, and very clever and intelligent."

The next day she sent him a note telling him that he had

"made a very favorable impression." Three days later she told Melbourne that she had changed her mind about getting married. Five days after that first dinner dance, she sum-

Prince Albert of Saxe-Coburg. *(Courtesy of Her Majesty the Queen.)*

moned Albert to court and told him "it would make me *too happy* if he would consent to what I wished." Victoria was proposing marriage.

A contemporary drawing depicting Victoria's proposal to Albert.

While Albert liked and respected Victoria, he had reasons to be wary about the marriage. He would have to leave his beloved birthplace of Coburg and become part of the social life of the English court though he preferred a quieter life in the country. He worried he would be unhappy at court, musing, "V. is said to be incredibly stubborn . . . she delights in court ceremonies, etiquette and trivial formalities. These are gloomy prospects." Still, he comforted himself with the thought the marriage would allow him to do good, "using his powers and endeavors for a great object—that of promoting the welfare of multitudes of his [new] countrymen." When he was eleven years old, Albert had resolved: "I intend to train myself to be a good and useful man." He never forgot that resolution. He told Victoria that he would be very happy to marry her. She confessed to her diary: "I feel the happiest of human beings."

Political advisors and family members on both sides agreed to the match and the engagement was announced on November 23, 1839. While most people were pleased at the news, some harbored suspicions about Albert's German heritage. A popular doggerel verse of the time said that Albert was:

> Come to take 'for better or worse'
> England's fat queen and England's fatter purse.

Although apparently smitten by Albert from the beginning, Victoria did have some doubts. She wrote: "I have always had my own way. . . . Suppose he should endeavor to thwart me." She told the Archbishop of Canterbury that she would promise to obey her husband "though not as a *queen,* as a *woman.*" The wedding was set for February 10, 1840.

Soon after the wedding was announced, an issue came up that would haunt the royal couple for years to come. Victoria had alienated the Tories early on with her support of the Whigs and during the Bedchamber Crisis. Now, when Victoria petitioned Parliament to have Albert made a British citizen, the Tories objected. She also needed to go through Parliament to have an official title for Albert approved. "Consort" was appended to the titles of those who entered the nobility or royalty through marriage. Victoria wanted Albert to be king consort. The Tories in Parliament refused—they did not want to cede anything to Victoria, nor did they want a foreigner to be called king. After extensive negotiations and many threats from Victoria, Albert was eventually named prince consort—which the queen felt was a stinging defeat. She spoke angrily of the "abominable, infamous Tories" but their message was clear: Victoria should have practiced greater diplomacy. For years to come, Albert would be hamstrung by his lack of official power.

A few days before the wedding Albert arrived at the port city of Dover. Cheering crowds lined his route to London. There the schedule called for him to visit with Victoria in her sitting room, where she awaited his arrival with her entire household. Legend says that the minute Victoria heard the carriages of Albert's procession she left the room and rushed downstairs to greet him personally with hugs and kisses.

One of the first things Victoria did on the morning of her wedding was to break a long-standing English tradition. She insisted on seeing her bridegroom before the ceremony. Then, at 12:30 she and her mother and several ladies-in-waiting left Buckingham Palace. The pouring rain did not deter the crowds standing along her route to the Chapel Royal. Victoria wore a white satin gown trimmed with lace, an orange-blossom wreath, and a magnificent sapphire and diamond brooch, a gift from Albert. Twelve children in white dresses trimmed with red roses carried her train. The groom wore his field marshal's uniform with enormous

Queen Victoria is credited with starting the trend of wearing a white wedding dress. Royal brides traditionally wore a brocade dress and a fur cloak.

white rosettes on the shoulders. After the short ceremony, the couple adjourned to a wedding breakfast at Buckingham Palace that featured a nine-foot-round cake weighing several hundred pounds. Hours of public appearances in front of cheering crowds followed.

The newlyweds had no honeymoon. Though Albert wanted one, Victoria reminded him that such a thing was impossible: "You forget, my dearest Love, that I am the sovereign, and that business can stop and wait for nothing." During the first weeks of their marriage, Victoria sent glowing notes to family and friends saying how she adored Albert. She planned several large parties, although she noted that Albert disliked meeting strangers. She tried to introduce him to his new country, but his stiff German bearing and discomfort with the English language did not endear him to the public.

When Victoria married Albert she married into her German mother's side of the family. At this time, Germany was still not yet a country, but a loose collection of states dominated by the largest, Prussia. Many people in Britain feared Prussia, which had a tradition of militarism and an eagerness to expand its territory. There was concern that Albert's influence would make the crown of England more sympathetic to Prussia.

Most people in Great Britain would eventually realize their fears about Albert were unfounded. He was a champion of reform and threw himself into campaigns against malnutrition and poor housing. Under his supervision, hundreds of public libraries, reading rooms, parks, and social clubs were created. Though Victoria supported Albert's efforts, she was not as eager for the kind of major changes that would require government intervention—or money.

Many of the services of government we take for granted today were unheard of in the 1830s. Water was not treated, and people threw their garbage into the streets where it rotted. The mentally ill were kept locked away in horrendous conditions, and prisons were little more than miserable, dangerous open camps surrounded by guards. What few schools existed for those who could not afford private tutors were generally run by churches and woefully understaffed. Midway through the century, a survey found that eighty percent of working-class children in London had never been to school. A slightly higher percentage outside the city went to school, but what education there was to be had was usually of very poor quality.

The passage of the Reform Act of 1832 did improve some of the worst injustices in how representatives were sent to

Parliament. It eliminated some of the "rotten boroughs" and created some new boroughs in underrepresented areas. But the right to vote was limited to landholders and most of the poor did not have the power of the ballot. Until they could vote, it would be difficult to get true reforms of child labor laws and other pressing social issues.

The Reform Act of 1832 was only passed after a great public outcry. There had been riots and marches in several cities after the act was initially defeated in 1831. It failed two more times and then finally passed after King William IV threatened to create dozens of new peerages to insure its passage in the more conservative House of Lords. After the 1832 reform bill, additional bills that slightly expanded the right to vote were passed.

Soon after Victoria became queen, however, it became clear that efforts to improve the lives of workers and the poor were moving too slowly. The Anti-Corn Law League was formed in 1839, around the time the Chartist movement was gaining strength. Both advocated for the passage of bills designed to improve the lot of the working and middle classes. These two organizations became the main voices for reform over the next few years.

The Anti-Corn Law League, which was primarily middle class, argued that the stiff import tariffs (taxes paid on goods brought into the country) imposed by the Corn Law of 1815 artificially inflated the price of grain and products made from grain, such as bread. They also argued that because so much of working people's money was being used to buy bread there was little left over to buy the goods manufactured in the new British factories. As the right to vote was slowly extended, the Anti-Corn Law League gained strength and influence. Nevertheless, it was not until seven years later that the tariffs on imported grain were lifted.

The Chartist movement sprang from something called the People's Charter, a document signed by hundreds of thousands of supporters and presented to Queen Victoria and Parliament. The Chartists focused on election reform. Their six main desires were: universal male suffrage, a secret ballot, no more unequal boroughs, annual Parliaments, the end of property qualifications for members of Parliament, and salaries for Parliament members so those who were not independently wealthy could serve. The Chartists grew rapidly in number and in volume. They held marches and rallies and advocated on the local and national level. But the movement was not popular with the middle class, which considered it a threat to their power. This lack of middle class support doomed the Chartists to failure. It would be years before all six of their points became law.

Prince Albert's enthusiasm for reform was partially a result of his inherent belief in fairness and civility. When Robert Peel returned as prime minister, members of both parties feared a rehashing of the infamous Bedchamber Crisis. Albert gained the support of both Melbourne and Victoria's old advisor Stockmar to enter into delicate negotiations with Peel's representatives about the problem of Victoria's ladies-in-waiting. They agreed that the Whig ladies should be replaced by Tory ladies when Peel took office and that the prime minister would make the appoint-

ments. During these negotiations, Albert and Peel discovered they had much in common. Both were naturally shy,
enjoyed the arts, and were concerned with the welfare of the
working people. Peel appointed Albert chairman of the
Royal Commission on the Fine Arts and the two men
discussed politics and art whenever they could find the time.
Albert's admiration for Peel helped Victoria to reconsider
her attitude toward the man she had found to be cold and
officious. She managed to be gracious at Peel's installation
ceremony, a fact noted with relief by both the court and
Parliament. Albert obviously had a steadying, calming
influence on his new wife.

5

Family and Home

Victoria and Albert were a happy, generally loving couple, but there were occasional arguments and even rumors of thrown lamps and slamming doors. Victoria confided in her journal that sometimes she failed to control her emotions: "There is often an irritability in me which . . . makes me say cross and odious things which I don't myself believe." The tantrums, which had been so famous when she was a girl, continued into adulthood: "How uncontrollable my temper is when annoyed and hurt," she wrote. Albert was usually patient with his wife, and like Louise Lehzen, tried to handle her outbursts with gentle kindness. But in the early years of their marriage, it was a conflict over Lehzen that was often at the heart of their arguments.

Since becoming queen and extricating herself from her mother's influence, Victoria had relied heavily on her be-

Baroness Louise Lehzen.

loved governess. One journal entry shows Victoria's feelings: "Walked with my ANGELIC, dearest Mother, *Lehzen*, who I do so love." Lehzen cared deeply for Victoria, too, and did her best to guide her former charge. However, Lehzen had no training to serve as private secretary to a queen. As she aged it became harder for her to oversee the complicated household. When he arrived at Buckingham Palace, Albert found things to be, in his estimation, poorly run. Much of the money being poured into the household—nearly 300,000 pounds a year went to the upkeep of the queen's properties—was finding its way into the wrong pockets.

Early on, Victoria refused to hear a word against Lehzen or her poor management. Albert stewed over the situation for several months before confronting her again. He told Victoria, gently but firmly, that it was time to let her nanny go. He laid down a list of grievances and proved irrefutably that money that could be saved and efficiency improved if Lehzen was replaced.

Among the data Albert brought to Victoria was the

alarming information that in one three-month period, Buckingham Palace served over 24,000 dinners to people the queen had never met. The servants were inefficient, as well as poorly paid. Stockmar pitched in with a report detailing some of the worst problems. One example he gave was the procedure for repairing a broken pane of glass in a pantry:

> A requisition is prepared and signed by the Chief Cook, it is then countersigned by the Clerk of the Kitchen, then it is taken to be signed by the Master of the Household, thence it is taken to the Lord Chamberlain's Officer where it is authorised, and then laid before the Clerk of the Works.

Victoria finally admitted the system needed an overhaul, and Lehzen was sent back to Germany with a stable retirement stipend.

Victoria's idea of a perfect evening was to dance throughout the night and then watch the sun rise from behind the Westminster towers. Albert preferred to converse with distinguished scholars and literary men and retire early. Victoria showed tolerance of religious views and practices. Albert was a strict Lutheran and intolerant of other beliefs. He was uncomfortable in large groups. One thing they did agree on was the importance of class distinctions. Both he and Victoria demanded respect be paid to their royal positions.

Though Albert was not king, he refused to be Victoria's subject. Once, after a quarrel, Albert retired early and locked his study door. Victoria pounded on the door. Albert

asked, "Who is there?" She answered, "The Queen." He did not respond. Time after time she pounded on the door and the same dialogue ensued. Finally in answer to Albert's question, Victoria answered, "Your wife." He opened the door and they reconciled. On another occasion Albert was at dinner

This watercolor portrait of Albert was painted by Victoria during the early years of their marriage.

when Victoria sent a note asking him to come home immediately. He read the note at the table, then folded it and went on with his conversation. She sent several more, increasingly angry, missives over the next few hours, and Albert ignored each one. When he adjourned for the evening, he asked his coachman to drive him to the couple's other castle where he passed a pleasant night before returning to Victoria the next morning. His message to her was clear.

In June of 1840, Albert saved Victoria's life. They were riding in an open carriage when a loud explosion startled them both. Albert was quick to realize it was a gunshot, and just before the would-be assassin fired again, Albert pushed Victoria to the floor of the carriage. This unfortunate event

This depiction of the assasination attempt made on Victoria in 1840 was drawn by a newspaper artist who did not know that the would-be assasin, Edward Oxford, was not a gentleman but a busboy at a local tavern.

rallied public opinion behind the queen and her prince. The people of England were furious that someone would try to murder their sovereign, and Albert's bravery was roundly cheered. The couple's public image got another boost with the announcement that the queen was expecting.

Victoria's first pregnancy was uneventful. As it progressed, she spent less time in public and more time in her private chambers. There she handled official correspondence and met with her ministers, Albert always by her side. Though he had no official position in the government, Victoria came to rely on his help. As her ministers soon realized, Albert was a thoughtful, wise, and insightful advisor. They too came to trust his good judgement, and soon the prince consort was fulfilling the role of the queen's private secretary.

On November 21, 1840, Princess Victoria, little Vicky, was born. The new parents wrote: "a perfect little child was born but alas a girl." Victoria spoke frankly about children: "I have no tender [tenderness] for them till they have become a little human; an ugly baby is a very nasty object— and the prettiest is frightful when undressed." Unlike many Victorian men, Albert was intensely interested in his baby. He spent time in the nursery with little Vicky and caring for Victoria. Soon after the baby's birth, Parliament designated Albert as regent should the queen die before her daughter was of age. Albert's regency passed through Parliament with only one dissenting vote—a tribute to his rising popularity.

The next year, 1841, Victoria faced two more assassination attempts. She shrugged off suggestions that she retreat behind guards or closed doors and continued to greet her subjects from open carriages and balconies. Her bravery endeared her to them even more. She did supervise the passing of a bill through Parliament that made attempts on the queen's life high misdemeanors, punishable by exile, imprisonment, or whipping. All told, Victoria would face seven assassination attempts during her long reign. In each case, the men were judged to be acting independently and almost all were found to be insane.

Later in 1841, Victoria took her first ride in a railroad car. She enjoyed the trip immensely. Victoria's historic ride marked the beginning of a new era—the dawn of railroad travel. Railroads would change her country more than any politician ever could. England's relatively small size (less than three percent of the area of the United States) meant railroads made an immediate change. People could travel for pleasure, and goods could easily be moved from one part of the country to another. England's advanced industry also made it the world leader in the production of railroad supplies, which were then shipped all over the globe.

As she settled into her new family, Victoria came to enjoy royal life more than ever. Her happiness was complete when she gave birth to her second child—this time, a son. Prince Albert Edward was born less than a year after his sister, in 1841. He was called Bertie, and from the moment of his birth he was groomed to be king.

From morning until night, Victoria conferred with the nannies about her children, worked on the business of state, and kept up with the baskets of dispatches sent to her. When necessary she left Windsor to travel to Buckingham Palace to open Parliament, interview members of the government, and entertain foreign visitors in splendor. She earned the admiration of the court for her energy and hard work. She had matured into a woman who seemed much different from the fun-loving, even frivolous, young queen. She was happy with the simple lifestyle she shared with Albert and their children. After rereading some of her journal entries written before she married Albert, she was amazed: "I cannot forebear remarking what an artificial sort of happiness *mine* was *then* and what a blessing it is I have now . . . *real* and solid happiness."

Victoria and Albert both liked to be away from London to enjoy the quiet and privacy of the country. They built a home for themselves on the Isle of Wight, at Osborne. The Osborne house was a perfect retreat—complete with tables and chairs specially sized to fit the petite queen. The house

Prince Albert himself designed the Osborne Palace, on the Isle of Wight, in the Italianate style.

had plenty of room for their growing family and the small army of nurses, nannies, tutors, and other servants who traveled with them.

All the staff in the world could not overcome the challenge presented by Bertie, however. As the boy grew older, his parents were disappointed to find that, unlike his older sister Vicky, Bertie was not a good student. His parents set out for him an ambitious curriculum of study and, while the boy tried to please them, his strengths were in his charm, not his intellect. Several times, Victoria and Albert changed Bertie's tutors, rescheduled his lessons, and revised his curriculum, all to no avail. Victoria wrote in her diary: "Poor Bertie! He vexes us much. There is not a particle of reflection, or even attention to anything but dress." Victoria and her son would have rocky relationship her entire life.

When Bertie was almost two and a half years old, and Vicky nearly three and a half, the twenty-three-year-old queen gave birth to another daughter, Princess Alice. Over the next fourteen years, there would be six more children.

This 1843 cartoon was entitled the "The Queen and Prince Albert at Home."

Amazingly, only one—Prince Leopold, born in April of 1853—had any health problems. He was a hemophiliac. After Alice's birth, the queen entered a period of depression. She was frustrated about having so many children and the toll each pregnancy took. The daughters would have to be found suitable marriages, and the sons supported for the rest of their lives. The old adage, "an heir and a spare," referred to the royal need for only two children—preferably both boys. This family, however, would eventually grow to nine.

6

Ireland

When Victoria became queen, Great Britain had been the dominant power in Ireland for centuries. In the sixteenth century, King Henry VIII broke with the Catholic Church and established the Protestant Church of England as the official state religion. The Irish population, meanwhile, remained overwhelmingly Catholic. After the break with Rome, the British government encouraged Protestant Englishmen to settle in Ireland. This led to a clash of religions and cultures. The Protestant English disliked the Catholic Irish, whom they considered to be little more than barbarians, and the Irish resented the British invaders.

In 1688, it became evident to most of the British aristocracy that their new king, James II, who had sworn to uphold the Church of England, was a secret Catholic. During his short reign he had attempted to push through a policy of religious toleration that most interpreted as an attempt to restore Catholic hegemony. The majority of Parliament and other nobles turned to William of Orange, who was married to the king's daughter Mary, both of whom were Protestant, and asked him to invade England, overthrow James, and rule jointly with his wife.

William invaded from Scotland and quickly defeated his father-in-law's dwindling forces. James fled to France, where he lived in exile for the rest of his life. Parliament decreed that James had abdicated the throne and crowned William and Mary as his successors. Parliament also took the opportunity to pass a series of laws now known as the Acts of Parliament that made the sovereign's power further subservient to the elected body. They also passed measures forbidding a Catholic from ever again coming to power in England. Catholics were not allowed to vote or hold office—even in Ireland, where some eighty percent of the population was Catholic. The result was minority rule in Ireland.

After the French Revolution in 1789, the Irish began to advocate for more independence from Britain. The English wanted to keep the Irish under tight control, partly because they reaped wealth from their farms and fisheries, and partly because they feared that Catholic France or Spain would use Ireland as a staging point for an invasion. Token measures toward self-rule were slowly granted to Ireland, however. When Victoria came to the throne, the Irish had their own Parliament, but resented that it had to meet at Westminster. They were also unhappy with the establishment of the

Church of England in Ireland, and the stringent Corn Laws. Under the command of the charismatic and dedicated leader Daniel O'Connell, the move toward Irish independence, or Home Rule, was growing stronger.

Political tensions were heightened when Ireland's potato crop failed in 1845. Since the potato had been brought over from North America, it had become a major food source in Ireland. In poorer areas, people relied almost solely on potatoes for food. In 1845, farm after farm found their crops covered in black rot. The fungus caused widespread poverty and starvation. It was one of the worst famines in recorded history. Farmers who counted on their crops for money to pay rent were evicted. Thousands of people died, while thousands more fled to England and America. In less than five years, the population of Ireland dropped from about eight million to about five million people.

Because of the influx of Catholic Irish immigrants in England, the pope took the unprecedented step of appointing a cardinal for Westminster Abbey. He made this decision without consulting either the queen, who was the official head of the Anglican Church, or the Archbishop of Canterbury, the top religious figure. While she favored religious freedom, Victoria was affronted by what she saw as a high-handed move. Whig leader Lord John Russell, who did not share the queen's commitment to religious freedom, went so far as to call the infusion of Catholic immigrants from Ireland a hostile act. He said it was part of a Catholic conspiracy to take over the nation. Although Victoria responded to this charge by saying, "I cannot bear to hear the violent abuse of the Catholic religion," she was torn between her desire to respect the right to worship and her own coronation vow to uphold the Church of England.

Between the Irish famine and the Catholic crisis, Prime Minister Robert Peel's government was faltering badly. Peel was a Tory, but he hoped focusing on social reform would gain him and his party some much-needed support from middle-class and other newly franchised voters. He threw his support behind repealing the Corn Laws and also initiated the Ten-Hour Bill, which would restrict child laborers to working no more than ten hours a day. This bill was unpopular with many merchants and factory owners. Peel's reformist zeal impressed the queen. Though Victoria had not wanted the Tories to take office five years earlier, now she hoped Peel would be able to stay in office until he was able to pass his reform agenda.

Peel continued to push for the repeal of the Corn Laws. He argued repeal was necessary to allow for grain to be more cheaply imported into Ireland and to alleviate the widespread starvation. But it was two more long years before the repeal passed. Both Peel and Victoria were frustrated at not being able to do more in the meantime. When the British Association for the Relief of the Extreme Distress in the Remote Parishes of Ireland and Scotland was formed, Victoria donated 2,000 pounds. She preached kindness: "To hear of their [the poor] wants and troubles, to minister to them, to look after them . . . It is there that you learn lessons of kindness to one another, of patience and endurance and resignation which cannot be found elsewhere."

Robert Peel, portrayed here standing at the center of the House of Commons, spent much of his tenure as prime minister embroiled in the Corn Law debate.

Victoria was given a chance to practice what she preached when she decided to visit Ireland in 1849, to meet the people there and to see their living conditions firsthand. Making the arrangements for her trip was tricky. The famine was not yet over and officials worried the amount of money spent to welcome her might create more hostility among the people.

Those officials need not have worried. Victoria's visit was a tremendous success. People came from all over the country; she spent hours being presented with thousands of citizens. Throughout her rigorous and demanding schedule, Victoria's energy never flagged. She was down-to-earth and gracious, and when she finally boarded the *Victoria and Albert,* a specially commissioned steam ship, to return home, she stood on the deck waving until the coastline was out of sight. Thousands of Irish waved back. There are historians who suggest that if the English government had been able to capitalize on the goodwill Victoria's visit created, the troubles between the two countries that followed might have been avoided.

In 1845, Victoria was pregnant again. As usual, her confinement meant she had to depend even more on Albert. Though Albert did everything he could to support Peel's government, he could not save the prime minister. Princess Helena was born on May 25, 1846, and Robert Peel resigned one month later. His resignation was made less painful because the hated Corn Laws had finally been repealed.

The end of Peel's government meant Victoria had to offer the position of prime minister to the Whig leader. Lord John Russell was a palatable candidate because he favored reform, but it was his foreign secretary, Lord Palmerston, who dominated his administration.

Palmerston was sixty-two years old when he became foreign secretary. He had a lifetime of experience in politics.

The *Victoria and Albert,* a specially commissioned steamship that transported Victoria to Ireland in 1849.

He was in favor of giving the vote to Catholics, and his family owned extensive estates in Ireland, in addition to their palatial family residence in England. Yet during the famine, Palmerston had hundreds of his Irish tenant farmers shipped to Canada to avoid having to feed and house them. Most arrived in terrible condition, barely clothed and having been poorly supplied with food. As many as a quarter of them died on the trip.

Palmerston was a man of contradictions. When he was shot in the shoulder by a soldier angry that he had advocated cuts to officer's pensions, Palmerston paid for the man's defense and made sure he was taken care of when sent to a mental hospital. But when a man was arrested for hunting illegally on his family's property, he did not intervene to save him from execution. He said that it would not be proper for him to use his personal influence. He was also notorious for his romantic entanglements with married women and was sued for adultery when he was seventy-eight years old.

Victoria did not like or approve of Palmerston. They clashed repeatedly. Russell, on the other hand, proved to be a responsible administrator. During his tenure as prime min-

Foreign Secretary, Lord Palmerston.

ister he helped pass legislation limiting working hours in factories, establishing a public health system, and repealing the navigation acts that restricted colonial trade. Despite these achievements, Russell's efforts to prevent widespread starvation in Ireland were unsuccessful.

In England, the decade of the 1840s came to be known as the Hungry Forties. In addition to the famine in Ireland, the Industrial Revolution brought millions of people into the cities, and many did not have enough to eat. Living conditions in the huge slums were horrific. There was raw sewage in the streets; disease was rampant. Victoria's glimpse of the squalor of a mining town appalled her, yet she realized it was "but a faint impression of the life which a third of a million of my poor subjects are forced to lead. It makes me sad."

Despite her sympathy, Victoria was never as committed to reform as Albert, or even some of her prime ministers. When some of the millions suffering from the potato famine in Ireland rebelled and attacked landlords there, Victoria said: "Really, they [the rebels] are a terrible people."

The 1840s was also the decade in which the Chartist movement reached its zenith. In the spring of 1848, the Chartists planned a major demonstration in London. Victoria's court was concerned for the queen's safety and decided she should leave the city—along with her newborn daughter, Princess Louise. While some in the court worried Victoria would earn the public's derision if she fled, most believed it was the prudent option. Victoria left London and a few days later over fifteen thousand British workers marched to Kensington to present a petition asking for legislation to regulate the wages and hours of working people and for the crown's help in obtaining better living conditions.

The government ordered soldiers into the city, worried the Chartists would turn violent. In the end, the march was peaceful, though that did not stop the government from charging three of its leaders with treason and sentencing them to death. Victoria had little sympathy for the would-be revolutionaries, declaring that "Obedience to the laws & to the Sovereign is obedience to a higher Power, divinely instituted for the good of the people." Though she had some sympathy for those less well off, Victoria's faith in the class system and her divine right as queen was never shaken.

7

Great Exhibition

The British had always benefited from geography. As an island separated from but in proximity to Europe, Great Britain, which included Wales and Scotland, had been protected from invasion by the English Channel. The British had been able to choose to disengage from European affairs, which led to a tradition of isolationism in British politics.

Because he was German, Prince Albert suffered more than a little abuse in newspapers and other places that trafficked in rumors. He was motivated to find a way to lessen this adherence to isolationism among the British. One of the ways he attempted to do this was through what he called a Great Exhibition. The purpose of the Great Exhibition was to present Great Britain to the world. His adopted country was the world leader in technological, industrial, and commercial development. How better to display these strengths than through a Great Exhibition that would attract visitors from around the globe? His hope was that displays of machinery and other inventions would convince foreign visitors of the great progress that could be made if peace was maintained. Ironically, it would also showcase Great Britain's empire, much of which was won and maintained by its superior army and navy.

For two years, Albert worked to gain the backing of manufacturers, colonial leaders, and ambassadors of foreign nations. In May 1851, the sixteen-acre Great Exhibition opened in Hyde Park, a public park in central London. There were huge crowds, bands, choirs, flags, and displays from a myriad of countries. Victoria and the royal children, dressed in kilts and frilly shirts and blouses, were cheered when they appeared at the gigantic glass and iron structure that Albert designed to house the exhibition. It was, in Victoria's words to her journal, "the *greatest* day in our history . . . the *happiest, proudest* day in my life."

There were over a hundred thousand exhibits. The lanes were lined with elm and palm trees; a huge crystal fountain was at the center of the hall. There were thousands of items on display: hats made of leaves plucked from Australian bushes, an alarm clock that tipped a lazy sleeper into a tub of cold water, a stove in the form of a knight in armor, stuffed animals posed like humans, a choir of six hundred, and an orchestra of two hundred. In all, there were over fourteen thousand exhibitors. About half were from abroad, including the American Cyrus McCormick, who showed up with his new invention—a horse-drawn mechanical reaper.

Onlookers standing in Hyde Park view the Crystal Palace at the Great Exhibtion.

Though the exhibition was popular with a majority of the British, some detractors, mostly aristocrats, complained that it was gaudy and ostentatious. Others complained that the money could be much better spent. A writer for the *Commonweal* said: "Now this monstrous stupidity [the exhibition] is on us . . . We must not after all forget what the hideous, revolting, and vulgar tomfoolery in question really means nowadays." Nevertheless, in the six months of its existence, over six million people visited the exhibition.

Albert's Great Exhibition was a social and cultural event, but it was also a symbolic show of political force. Europe was still reeling from the revolutions of 1848, which had spread rapidly across the continent, creating riots and toppling governments. Britain was the only major power to have weathered 1848 relatively unscathed—but the political situation was still tenuous. It is possible that Britain survived revolutionary fever because its government was more bureaucratic. Rulers in France, the German states, Austria, Hungary, Bohemia, and Italy were all challenged by citizens who wanted a more representative, parliamentary government. While Great Britain had its share of domestic problems and Parliament was always slow to react to calls for reform, the country's large, decentralized government protected it from the ire of a focused group of angry and disenfranchised citizens.

By the end of 1848, the queen, who was not yet thirty years old, had given birth to her sixth child in eight years. In November, former Prime Minister Melbourne, the queen's first advisor and trusted friend, died. While seeking solace for her grief in the countryside, the queen arranged to purchase an estate in Scotland called Balmoral. It was located in a wild, remote place, which suited her desire to be away from London. She loved the cold Scottish air and took her family there as often as possible.

Balmoral Castle.

At Balmoral, Victoria learned to like bannock, a Scottish griddlecake made with oatmeal or wheat flour, and to appreciate Highland people and their customs. Sometimes she would sit in a rowboat for hours while Albert fished for trout. They played outdoor games with the children, and enjoyed the natural setting. She admitted to her journal that she could hardly bear the trip back to England whenever they had to return.

In 1849, Victoria had more sad news. Former Prime Minister Peel died after his horse slipped on wet cobblestones and fell on him. She mourned his passing, but it was Albert who was most affected—Peel had become like a father figure to him. The birth of their seventh child, Prince Arthur, in the spring of 1850, did little to lift the pall that had settled over the royal household. Then there was more trouble with Foreign Minister Palmerston, as the Don Pacifico affair captured the nation's attention.

Don Pacifico was a British citizen living in Greece when his house there was robbed. His complaints to the Greek government were ignored. Seeking redress, Pacifico wrote to Palmerston who, acting on his own authority, sided with Pacifico and ordered British gunships to seize Greek shipping as a way to provide Pacifico reimbursement. Palmerston's action caused international outrage; Victoria was furious when she heard what he had done. She insisted that Prime Minister Russell remove Palmerston from his post.

Before Russell could act, Palmerston went before Parliament and made a passionate speech defending his actions.

He told his listeners that British citizens everywhere should be able to rely on the full protection of their government. A brilliant piece of oratory, Palmerston's jingoistic speech swayed public opinion after it was printed in newspapers and on leaflets. The foreign minister became so popular, so quickly, Russell could not fire him. Victoria was livid.

Palmerston next directly contradicted Victoria's orders in a very public fashion. In 1851, Louis Napoleon overthrew the French government that had been established after the 1848 revolution. A nephew of Napoleon Bonaparte, Louis had himself crowned Emperor Napoleon III. Though many in Britain were sympathetic to Louis Napoleon's cause, the British government could not support the overthrow of a constitutional government. Relations between France and England had been tense for months, although Victoria had made diplomatic progress with the ousted King Louis Philippe. Officially, Britain planned to remain neutral on French domestic politics. Palmerston, however, assured the French that Victoria, and the British government, endorsed the new government.

This time, Prime Minister Russell was as angry as the queen. Though he knew it meant the end of his ministry, Russell had Palmerston removed from office. As expected, Russell's government failed and eventually a new one was formed around the Earl of Aberdeen. The new prime minister wanted to make Palmerston foreign minister again, but Victoria managed to block the appointment. Palmerston was relegated to the role of Home Secretary. The queen seethed to see him in any position of power.

8

Pax Britannica

Great Britain had the world's preeminent navy during the nineteenth century. This, combined with the wealth that flowed into the country from industrial development, banking, and other types of commerce, had made the relatively small island nation the most powerful country in the world by the middle of the century. This was also the age of imperialism, as wealthy European nations began to colonize less developed regions, such as sub-Saharan Africa and great sections of Asia.

In the Middle East and Central Europe, the dominant power had long been the Ottoman Empire of Turkey. A great deal of the Islamic world was at one point controlled by Turkey. However, Ottoman power had been in decline after several costly wars for independence in the seveneenth and eighteenth centuries. In addition to the internal problems

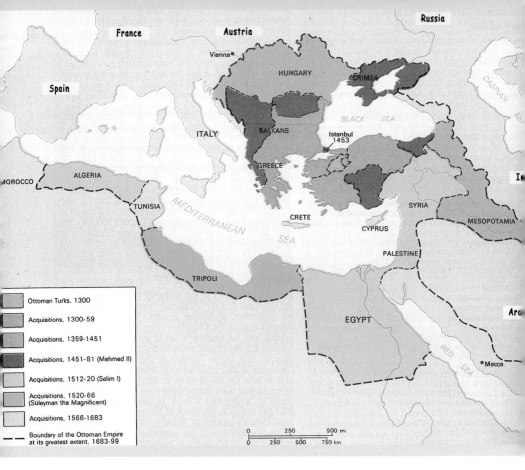

Legend:

- Ottoman Turks, 1300
- Acquisitions, 1300-59
- Acquisitions, 1359-1451
- Acquisitions, 1451-81 (Mehmed II)
- Acquisitions, 1512-20 (Selim I)
- Acquisitions, 1520-66 (Süleyman the Magnificent)
- Acquisitions, 1566-1683
- -- Boundary of the Ottoman Empire at its greatest extent, 1683-99

This map of the Ottoman Empire shows its various possessions from 1300-1699.

posed by administering such a large area filled with a wide assortment of ethnic and religious groups, the Turks had to contend with the growing power of Russia to the north. The Russians were motivated by the need for a warm water port, from which their naval and merchant ships could sail in the middle of the long Russian winter. The Austrian-Hungarian Empire was also trying to expand its influence into the Balkan Peninsula, where it competed with both the Turks and the Russians for hegemony. By the middle of the nineteenth century the once great Ottoman Empire was dubbed the "The Sick Man of Europe." The squabble that ensued as various European powers attempted to grab their piece of the decaying Ottoman Empire was the cause of most of the conflicts occupying Europe until the beginning of World War I in 1914 and even beyond. (The Balkan conflicts of the 1990s and the current tensions in the Middle East both involve areas once controlled by the Ottoman Empire.)

In 1853, Russian Czar Nicholas I decided the time was right to attempt to gain control of the Bosporus Straits, which linked the European part of Turkey to the Asian part. Controlling the straits would give Russia access to, and naval dominance of, the profitable Eastern Mediterranean trade routes. Russia had not matched the industrial development of Great Britain, Germany, and other European nations. Russia had few railroad lines and could not move troops or supplies quickly on land. The Czar decided to attack the Turkish fleet on the Black Sea.

Czar Nicholas I of Russia.

The British ambassador to the Ottomans, who resided in the capital city of Constantinople (now Istanbul), encouraged the Turks to stand up to the Russians. He feared that if Russian forces seized Constantinople they would pose a threat to British-controlled India. The ambassador was acting contrary to the orders he had received from Parliament when he encouraged the Turks to fight, but it took weeks for anyone in Britain to find this out—there was no quick way to get information fifteen hundred miles across Europe. By the time his bosses in London learned what had happened, it was too late. The ambassador had committed them to come to the aid of Turkey.

Appalled at the idea of a possible British intervention in a distant war, Victoria asked Czar Nicholas to settle the conflict. But he would not be deterred. British generals were sent to assess the situation. They reported back that the Turkish army was in shambles and British forces would have to do most of the fighting. But, even before their reports reached London, events took on their own momentum. Anti-Russian feeling ran high in Britain, where people had long feared the expansion of the huge Eurasian country. If Russia had easy access to either the Baltic or the Black Sea—and thus into the Mediterranean—it could threaten British naval superiority. On February 28, 1854, Parliament voted to declare war on Russia.

British military leaders devised a plan they were certain would bring easy victory. They would concentrate their forces on the port of Sevastopol, the chief base of the Russian Black Sea fleet. If their fleet could be bottled up and defeated, the Russians would have no choice but to retreat. Sevastopol is a large Ukrainian port city, located on the Crimean Peninsula. Thus began the Crimean War.

This painting depicts the charge of the light cavalry brigade at Balaclava on October 25, 1854. British poet Tennyson would describe the event with the haunting lines, "Into the valley of Death / Rode the six hundred."*(Courtesy of Art Resource.)*

Uneasy about taking on the fight alone, the British turned to an unlikely ally for help. Emperor Napoleon III of France hoped to profit in land and influence in the Middle East by defeating the Russians. For the first time in history, British troops allied with the French against a common enemy. The goal of both the French and the British was less the defense of Turkey than it was taking advantage of an opportunity to weaken Russia.

In September 1854, French and British troops began an assault on the Crimean Peninsula. Their intent was to gain a foothold from which to attack Sevastopol. In October 1854, a British brigade made a poorly planned attack on the harbor at Balaclava. Inept battlefield leadership, poor preparations, and shoddy communications culminated in the infamous Charge of the Light Brigade, which was immortalized in a poem by the British Poet Laureate Lord Alfred Tennyson. Almost seven hundred British cavalry soldiers were ordered to charge a heavily fortified Russian position. Less than two hundred survived. Incredible courage and a staggering disregard for life characterized the Crimean War. At one point, out of desperation, the Russians would even sink their own fleet to block the entrance to the Sevastopol harbor.

After the first few months of fighting, during which each side could have conceivably turned the war in its favor, winter set in and made warfare almost impossible. The British and French troops had no choice but to try to hold out until spring.

Victoria followed the events in the Crimea closely. She was appalled to learn about the conditions the British troops endured during that long winter. They were poorly supplied. Four times as many died from disease as did from enemy fire. By the time huts, food, and medicine arrived from England it was too late. One regiment, which normally had over one thousand members, was reduced to seven. Members of the House of Commons demanded an investigation into the conditions British soldiers faced in the Crimea. As a result of the furor, Prime Minister Aberdeen resigned. Though it rankled her to do so, Victoria had no choice but to appoint her old enemy Palmerston as his replacement.

When wounded soldiers returned to England, Victoria visited as many as possible and was generous in her praise of their patriotism and courage. They told her appalling stories of suffering from wounds, exhaustion, vermin, di-

Victoria and her family meeting the Grennadier Guards after their return from the Crimean War.

arrhea, and cholera. She spent time with Florence Nightingale, a British nursing pioneer, and learned from her about the best treatments for wartime injuries and sicknesses.

Victoria's journal was filled with entries recorded after these visits. "One man who had lost his arm . . . a private, Lanesbury, with a patch over his eye and his face tied up . . . I cannot say how touched and impressed I have been by the sight of these noble brave." In 1856, she instituted the Victoria Cross, an ornate medal and ribbon awarded to soldiers who performed an outstanding act of bravery or devotion. Prince Albert worked behind the scenes to fight against bureaucratic obstruction, corruption, and inertia, and to urge departments of the government to work harder and more cooperatively to end the war as soon as possible.

Sevastopol, the great Russian fortress in the Crimea, finally fell in September 1855. Though it would be six months before a peace treaty was signed, the fighting was effectively over. Nearly half the British troops sent to the Crimea did not return. As the fighting dwindled to a close, Victoria had to admit that Palmerston's management of the war effort had been instrumental in achieving peace. She invested in him the Order of the Garter, one of the highest honors she could bestow.

Plans between France and Great Britain for peace needed to be made, so in 1855, Emperor Louis Napoleon III arranged to visit London. Victoria agreed to make a visit of her own to Paris. This thank you for French support in the war would lend credence to his government. Privately, based on reports she had received, Victoria considered Napoleon III to be greedy and immoral. After meeting him, she was pleasantly surprised and impressed by his quiet manners and intelligent conversation. Victoria also liked Napoleon's wife, Eugénie. The two made an interesting picture: Victoria, stout and red-faced at the slightest exertion, dressed in

From left to right, Prince Albert, Empress Eugénie, Victoria, and Napoleon III during the queen's trip to Paris. *(Courtesy of Getty Images.)*

garish inexpensive garments including a purple pork-pie hat; Eugénie, slim and elegant, dressed in the latest European style with luxurious flounces and crinolines.

Victoria's return visit to Paris was also a success. Before long, Great Britain and France enjoyed the best political relationship in their history. Unfortunately, the end to the Crimean War did not lead to other happy results. The Treaty of Paris failed to resolve any of the issues brought forward by the deterioration of the Ottoman Empire, which was temporarily propped up by the Russian defeat. Essentially, the situation was not much changed. Russia was temporarily restrained, but the hunger for expansion still occupied European attention.

Just as events were winding down in the Crimea, the British were faced with more trouble. This time the problem was in its most prized possession—India.

Indian soldiers, who worked for the British government, had long been bitter about their meager wages. British officers had reported home for months that the relationship between them and their Indian troops was growing worse. This tense situation turned violent as the result of an inadvertent cultural insult.

The immediate cause, the spark that set off the Indian Mutiny, grew out of a problem with the manufacture of the cartridges the Indian soldiers were given for their guns. The cartridges were coated in grease made from pigs and cows. Cows, however, are sacred animals to many Hindus, and Muslims consider pigs unholy creatures. The vast majority of Indians were either Hindu or Muslim. Because the

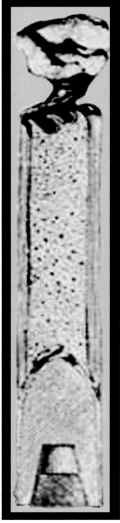

An Enfield cartridge.

cartridge packages were usually opened by ripping them with the teeth, the soldiers refused to use the cartridges. This insubordination led to a conflict between the officers and the soldiers that escalated into an open rebellion. By time the British military leaders in India realized their mistake, it was too late: they had a full-scale mutiny on their hands.

British involvement in India stretched all the way back to the beginning of the modern era. In 1612, the English East India Company had founded the first British trading post in India at Surat, on the Gulf of Khambhat. The company steadily expanded its operations, fighting off competition and threats from Dutch, Portuguese, and French traders, as well as from the Indians themselves. In addition to being an important trading partner, and a resource for cotton, tea, spices, and other valuable products, India became a safety valve for the British population explosion. In 1773, the East India Company became a semiofficial agency of the British government and, with the cooperation of the crown, made improvements to the Indian infrastructure and communication systems. But along with these physical improvements came bribery, extortion, and political manipulation. This political corruption, combined with the continuing hunger and poverty of most Indians, slowly turned popular opinion against the British.

As the native population became more and more dissatisfied, Britain stationed 40,000 soldiers in the country. These troops were often outnumbered by twenty to one. The dam broke in February 1857, in the dispute over the cartridges. The Indian Mutiny was an attempt to reject British rule. The rebel soldiers committed atrocities on British soldiers and subjects, and the British responded in kind. The country was wracked with fighting—people were tortured, drowned, shot, and even set on fire. The queen protested the atrocities on both sides, calling them "too horrible and really quite shameful." She kept careful tabs on the events in India,

The British punished the insurgents of the Indian Mutiny with a vengeance.

though she was once again recovering from childbirth—Princess Beatrice, her ninth and last child, was born in April of 1857.

In the fall of that same year, as the British were finally regaining control in India, Victoria issued a proclamation stating that in the future the British government would act with tolerance and conciliation to protect native religions and customs. She told the Indian people "that there is no hatred of brown skin, none; but the greatest wish on their Queen's part to see them happy, contented, and flourishing." She insisted that perpetrators of terror be arrested and punished severely, but that no innocent person should suffer in a frenzy to extract revenge. Though Victoria's attitude seemed reasonable, if not lenient, she had no intention of pulling out the troops. She said, simply, "India shd [should] belong to me."

In 1858, the government of India was transferred from the control of the East India Company to the British crown. Under the Better Government of India Act passed that year, British rule was tightened and a rigid bureaucracy was created. A viceroy appointed by the crown administered the entire country. Aware that British intolerance of indigenous religions had sparked the rebellion, Victoria insisted on a strict policy of religious freedom. When, in 1876, Victoria was declared empress of India, her first declaration after receiving the title was to make clear to all British officers abroad that they should treat natives "with every kindness and affection, as brothers, not—as alas! Englishmen too often do—as totally different beings to ourselves."

A Ruler Alone

During the years 1858 and 1859, the Thames River, which flows through central London, became so polluted with sewage that it was almost unbearable to be near it. The odor, which came to be known as the "Great Stink," was so strong that people who needed to cross the river would leave the city to cross upstream. Parliament could convene only if cloth soaked in a strong cleaning solution was hung over the windows. All boating on the river ceased.

This problem of unsanitary water made diseases, including typhoid and cholera, all too common. In addition to raw sewage, leaky caskets buried in overcrowded graveyards polluted the ground water. The connection had not yet been made between unclean water and disease. Most people, particularly in the lower classes, bathed infrequently. Contaminated drinking water was the norm. One third of all

The royal family on the occasion of Victoria's birthday. From left to right, Leopold, Louise, the queen, Arthur, Alice, Vicky, Beatrice, Albert, Helena.

British infants did not survive to the age of five.

Not surprisingly, Queen Victoria's family fared better than most. All of her children lived to adulthood and the queen herself had survived her bout with what was probably typhoid as a teenager. However, despite their elevated position, the queen's family still suffered from the inadequate infrastructure. When the Thames overflowed its banks, the lawn at Windsor was covered in raw sewage.

The one member of Victoria's family who proved most susceptible to disease was Albert. When his health first began to fail, Victoria thought his symptoms were the result of a bad fall from his carriage. Then he suffered a violent bout of vomiting and fever and could hardly sleep because of severe rheumatic pains. By early December of 1861, Albert was unable to hide his weakness from the public. He was diagnosed with the dreaded typhoid. Albert received the best possible medical care but there was little that could be done. On December 14, 1861, he died.

Prince Albert's death was a terrible blow to Victoria, one from which, in many ways, she did not recover. She had grown to depend on him as she made decisions and dealt with governmental leaders. Together they had seen her country through difficult and dangerous times. In her grief, she could hardly summon the energy to leave her rooms. The country mourned Albert's passing, too. Parliament finally gave official recognition to the unofficial role Albert had played for his adopted country: a member read out a declaration saying, "We have buried our sovereign. This German prince has governed England for twenty-one years with wisdom and energy."

Victoria was devastated. The few journal entries she made during this time reveal her despair: "I have no rest, no real rest or peace by day or by night: I sleep, but

This photograph, taken soon after Albert's death, shows the construction of the mausoleum in which he would be buried.

in such a way as to be more tired of a morning than at night and waken constantly with a dreamy, dreadful confusion of something having happened and crushed me." Physical illness weakened her. She told her diary her many symptoms: "My pulse gets so high, it is constantly between 90 and 100 instead of being at 74! . . . It exhausts me so and I am so weak and then my poor memory fails me so terribly." She was restless at night, writing many mornings that she had "scarcely got any sleep." She told everyone: "For me, life came to an end on 14 December."

Worried about his niece, King Leopold wrote that he was coming to visit. Victoria feared that Leopold would try to resume the role of her advisor and wrote back angrily, "*no human power* will make me swerve from *what he* [Albert] decided and wished." Stunned, Leopold aborted his plans for a visit. Victoria now had only two goals in life. One was to carry on Albert's work, and the other was to keep his memory alive in the minds and hearts of the English people.

Someone in the court remembered Victoria's fondness for a gruff stableman in the royal household at Balmoral. His name was John Brown. He was quickly brought from Scotland, along with the queen's favorite pony. Brown was one of the few people who was able to give Victoria comfort. He had been an attendant during many happy family excursions in Scotland. He was there to help Victoria when the ground was rough, to remind her to wear a shawl as the temperature cooled, and to fix her tea with whiskey at the end of a day. The man and the pony raised her spirits a little, enough for her to say that Brown was "a *real* comfort, for

Victoria on horseback with John Brown.

he is *so* devoted to me . . . and so cheerful and attentive."

While Victoria's devotion to Albert's memory was clear, rumors about her relationship with John Brown began to spread. He accompanied Victoria everywhere and served as her personal attendant. Reports of their closeness offended her children, alienated some of her close attendants, and fueled court gossip. In popular jokes, she was called Mrs. John Brown. It was unthinkable to her family and subjects that the widowed queen would have a romantic interest, although the double standard of the day put no such restriction on a king, whether widowed or not.

Brown continued to serve the queen loyally and made no attempts to push himself into politics or other roles for which he was not considered suitable. Over time, most people came to accept him for what Victoria insisted he was—the only person she could trust, and a servant who devoted his life to his queen. John Brown would die unexpectedly on Easter 1883, and Victoria would be shattered by the loss. After his death, she wrote pages of letters to her family, in which she sobbed, "Now all, all is gone in this world . . . [Brown] was the truest and most devoted of all!"

For the decade after Albert's death, Victoria was probably what we today would consider clinically depressed. Her thoughts were dominated by the idea that her life was over. She indulged herself in self-pity, to the extent that she exhausted the support her children and others had to offer. To her closest aides she admitted she did not always think clearly. Rumors spread that the queen was descending into madness; those who remembered the reign of her grandfather, George III, shuddered at the thought of another lunatic Hanoverian.

Throughout the 1860s Victoria suffered from fatigue, listlessness, irritability, anxiety, nausea, and headaches. Her doctors generally agreed with whatever distressing news Victoria gave them about her illnesses, secretly attributing many of her problems to self-centered obsession.

Victoria's prolonged mourning confused her ministers and aides. They were used to a demanding and intelligent queen who wanted to know every detail of their business. The public missed the pageantry of the throne, and high society missed the balls and other entertainment that had become frequent in court. Sales in dresses, hats, and other fineries dropped. As time went on, public dissatisfaction with Victoria's behavior grew. The press was rude, and

Bertie, the Prince of Wales, as he looked in his twenties.

leaders of foreign nations voiced outright skepticism about the power and authority of Britain. Through it all, Victoria maintained her right to mourn her beloved husband and to carry on Albert's work in her own way. She was "a cruelly misunderstood woman," she told a journalist. She insisted it was not "the Queen's *sorrows* that keeps her secluded . . . It is her *overwhelming work* and her health."

Gradually, through necessity more than desire, Victoria was brought back into the public realm. Her eldest son Albert Edward, called Bertie, was twenty-three years old. He seemed to care for little but drinking, hunting, good food, and, most of all, pursuing actresses. Victoria urgently wanted Bertie to marry. She believed it would calm him down. She knew the bride would have to be beautiful and dutiful as well as Protestant. Victoria settled on Princess Alexandra of Denmark. The marriage was arranged and a wedding was held in March of 1863. Within six years they had five children, including two sons.

The public continued to stew over the queen's extended

Bertie and Alexandra with their five children on board the royal yacht *Osborne*. *(Courtesy of Getty Images.)*

mourning period. It might be appropriate for most wealthy widows, but was totally inappropriate for a queen who was expected to work hard. After all, she was certainly paid well. The queen drew a salary of nearly 400,000 pounds a year from the taxpayers. Some journalists suggested that she retire from the throne if she was unwilling or unable to fulfill her responsibilities. She was criticized for not allowing Bertie to perform her royal functions. It was publicly suggested that she abdicate in favor of the prince.

Victoria refused to consider giving up her job as queen.

Although Albert had insisted she make no images of him after he died, she commissioned a large number of models, paintings, and statues. At Frogmore, near Windsor, she constructed a vast and elaborate mausoleum for herself and Albert. She also built the Victoria and Albert Museum in south Kensington, a complex of museums and institutions.

Finally, in 1866, five years after Albert's death, Victoria unwillingly gave in to the public agitation about her self-imposed exile. She agreed to open Parliament, a traditional annual ceremony. She presided at the ceremony but refused to drive there in the government coach or to read the prepared speech. She merely sat, stoutly rigid, and stared. The next day she described herself as "terribly shaken, exhausted, and unwell from the violent *nervous* shock" of her appearance.

It would take another powerful and charismatic figure to bring the queen back into politics. When she was crowned, at the tender age of eighteen, it was the fatherly Lord Melbourne who guided her through the intricacies of government. Albert had been a steadying force, gamely providing behind-the-scenes advice during nearly twenty-two years of marriage. After his death, the queen was adrift for several years until the brilliant politician Benjamin Disraeli entered her world.

Disraeli was a unique figure in British politics. Although he later converted to Anglicanism, Disraeli was the son of a prominent Jewish family. He had traveled widely in his youth, and had abandoned a career in law in order to become a writer. Disraeli wrote several novels, but could not resist the pull of politics. His early political ventures were in keeping with his personality. He and the famous Irish leader Daniel O'Connell were once within minutes of fighting a duel after each had insulted the other's ancestors. Disraeli became famous for his smart, witty re-

Benjamin Disraeli.

marks and his grace in social situations. He enjoyed dressing well and was a much sought-after dinner guest. Despite his devil-may-care flair, Disraeli was also a serious politician who, although a member of the more conservative Tory Party, was committed to reform.

In 1867, thanks largely to Disraeli's efforts, another important Reform Bill was passed. This bill extended the franchise to nearly two million predominantly working-class males. The Tories supported the bill because they hoped most of those two million new votes would be cast for Tory candidates in the next election. The Reform Bill had originally been sponsored by the Reform League, which focused on securing the vote for all men, regardless of their education or wealth. Its members were often contentious, storming the gates of Hyde Park, knocking down light posts and setting fire to the gas pipes beneath them. Though Victoria distrusted this type of social activism—she tended to take it as a personal insult—she was liberalizing her attitude toward the British class system, saying "The Lower Classes are becoming so well-informed—are so intelligent & earn their bread & riches so deservedly that they cannot & ought not be kept back."

Although Victoria came to support offering the vote to a broader class of men, she insisted that the emerging feminist movement, which was initially centered primarily around winning women the right to vote, was "mad and utterly demoralizing." The women's suffrage movement in Britain began in the middle of the nineteenth century, but significant gains were not made until 1918. Despite her unusual status as the queen of an enormous empire, Victoria persisted in her belief that that women were less able than men in the world of government and politics. She declared publicly, "let women be what God intended; a helpmate for a man—but with totally different duties and vocations."

The passage of the Reform Bill helped vault Disraeli to the position of prime minister when the Tories came to power in 1868. He stayed in that office for only a year before his efforts to further enfranchise the working classes failed and he was forced out. The new Liberal Party, which had come into existence in 1859 and quickly replaced the Whigs as the Tories' main opposition party, elected a powerful majority in the House of Commons. Disraeli's archrival, William Gladstone, the leader of the Liberals, became the next prime minister.

Gladstone, who had been a leading government figure for decades, since before Victoria was crowned, was in many ways the opposite of Benjamin Disraeli. Where Disraeli was witty, Gladstone was dull. Disraeli was a consummate politician, gifted with a silver tongue and an opportunistic flair. He was always happy to accommodate people if it would help him to succeed. Gladstone was a steady worker, sober and serious, devoutly Christian and unafraid to force his moral judgements on anyone. He refused to flatter the queen and was even known to lecture her when he thought it necessary. He matched her in stubbornness. Victoria dreaded each meeting with Gladstone. His formal, long-winded speeches wearied her. "He speaks to me as if I were a public meeting," she complained. But the real rift between Victoria and

William Gladstone.

Gladstone opened in 1866 when he rose in Parliament and spoke against a request she had made for money to erect yet another statue of her late husband. While Gladstone tried to deny her the funds, Disraeli shrewdly worked to obtain them. Disraeli gained the queen's favor, and Gladstone lost it forever.

Over the course of thirteen years, Disraeli and Gladstone alternated holding the highest political office in the land. Though their policies were not always radically different, they disliked each other deeply on a personal level. The one out of power did his best to make the other's job difficult. Disraeli held office twice, for a total of nearly seven years. Gladstone, much to the queen's chagrin, had to be appointed four times, over a period of twenty-six years, and he served as prime minister for almost thirteen years. One thing both men had in common was impatience at Victoria's attempts to influence the government; but each man handled her differently. Disraeli preferred to flatter the queen and made a special effort to win her support by keeping her informed on select matters. Gladstone treated the queen like an intruder. She resented what she saw as his lack of concern for her wishes, and responded by peppering him with thousands of letters and notes.

Gladstone was committed to reform. His special interest was to bring stability, and eventually Home Rule, to Ireland. One of Gladstone's most peculiar habits was to walk the most seedy London streets at night, trying to persuade prostitutes to abandon their lives and to start new ones at the halfway house he and his wife had built. He also supported better education and fairer Parliamentary elections, including extending the right to vote to all men. Some of Gladstone's most important governmental achievements came before he was prime minister, when he was Chancellor of the Exchequer—the cabinet minister responsible for the budget. Gladstone developed a sound fiscal policy and modernized budgeting and accounting procedures. His hope was to improve efficiency as a way to better help the poor. A dedicated reformer domestically, where he attempted to put in place his ideas of Christian charity, Gladstone was more conservative when it came to England's foreign policy. He resisted the imperialist urge of most members of the Liberal Party, and favored a more isolationist policy. In general, his administrations focused on solving problems at home by making government more efficient and by increasing the freedoms and economic well-being of the average Briton.

During his political career, Disraeli also supported reform causes, including the Chartist movement, and he shared the queen's devotion to religious tolerance. But his real impact was in foreign affairs. Like the queen, Disraeli believed that Britain should have a more important international presence. Though he was not as devoted to imperialist expansion as Victoria was, Disraeli used her interest and support of an aggressive foreign policy to win her favor and her support for his reform policies at home.

10

Home Rule

Since Victoria's historic 1849 visit to Ireland, little had happened to improve the lives of the Irish people. In the long run, the repeal of the Corn Laws had actually hurt farmers. Cheap imported wheat, primarily from the United States, flooded into the country. Those farmers who could not lower their prices enough to compete with cheap wheat were forced off their land, usually by English landlords. This reinvigorated the calls for separation from Great Britain. Irish nationalists insisted that Ireland be given what they called Home Rule. The formidable Charles Stewart Parnell, who was actually a Protestant of English descent, emerged as the political leader of the Home Rule movement and rallied thousands to his side. Parnell did not advocate violence; instead he advocated using legal and political channels. Because he was Protestant, Parnell could serve in

Parliament. There he was highly skilled at keeping the cause of Home Rule in the forefront of debate and discussion.

William Gladstone worked closely with Parnell. Though they differed in personality, both of the men were dedicated, serious leaders. Parnell would eventually be forced out of office because of a long-running affair he had with a married woman.

Gladstone initiated a series of sweeping reforms, most of them aimed at bringing peace to Ireland. But legislation in London did little to improve the situation in Ireland. A worsening depression complicated by another famine led to murders, arson, and general mayhem.

Victoria was not as sympathetic to the plight of the Irish as Gladstone was. She called the Irish an impossible people and argued that in Ireland "the law is openly defied, disobeyed, and such an example may spread to England." She scolded Gladstone for his attempts to placate the Irish and blamed him for the violence. She became convinced there was no pleasing the Irish, who she saw as ungrateful, and that the only thing they understood was force. She voiced regret at not coming to this conclusion sooner and wrote to Gladstone regarding the troubles in Ireland: "If there are not sufficient soldiers to perform the duties required of them, let more regiments be sent. If the law is powerless to punish wrong-doers, let increased powers be sought."

The problem of Ireland became the most intractable of the era. (It would not be solved until after World War I, and remnants of it continue to this day in Northern Ireland.) Several of Gladstone's administrations collapsed because

The issue of Home Rule was a heated one in Ireland. This 1886 etching shows the Royal Irish Constabulary protecting a government reporter at a meeting of Charles Stewart Parnell's supporters.

his stance on Ireland was too extreme for most members of the Liberal Party. The Tories were even more opposed to the idea of Home Rule. Though he did not have the full support of his party, during his third term Gladstone again proposed Home Rule. He also suggested that Irish members of Parliament should meet in their home country instead of having to travel to Westminster as required by English law. Disregarding Albert's earlier warnings and the unspoken rule that queens should be party neutral, Victoria fought a frantic campaign to thwart Gladstone on the Irish question. She was convinced his policies would spell disaster for England.

On the day Gladstone's Irish bill was presented in Parliament, he addressed the assembly: "Ireland stands at your bar, expectant, hopeful, almost suppliant. . . . think, I beseech you, think well, think wisely, not for the moment, but for the years that are to come."

Despite this plea, the Home Rule Bill was defeated by thirty votes. Gladstone had no choice but to ask the queen to dissolve his government. Victoria accepted his resignation in a brief meeting, during which she granted him the title of earl—a token acknowledgment for his many years of service to the country. Irish members of Parliament continued to meet at Westminster, many of them making speeches full of ominous threats about the future relationship of Ireland and Great Britain. Victoria wrote in her journal: "The behavior of the Irish in the House of Commons is simply dreadful. . . . The Irish hope to force Home Rule by making themselves as disagreeable as possible." Her common complaint about Gladstone was expressed again in a letter to her daughter Vicky: "I feel very deeply that my opinion and my advice are never listened to [by Gladstone] and that it is almost useless to give any."

Gladstone never gave up on Home Rule. In his eighties, he returned to politics and reminded Parliament that he had vowed to see control of Ireland returned to the Irish people. In 1892, he took office as prime minister for the fourth time. Victoria was furious to see her old antagonist returned to power. Privately she raged at the idea that the government would once again be put "into the shaking hand of an old, wild, and incomprehensible man of 82 ½."

In early 1893, Home Rule was passed by the House of Commons but rejected by the House of Lords. Gladstone had failed again. He handed in his resignation in March 1894. Scrupulously honest as always, the queen worded her acceptance of his resignation in such a way that she could thank him for his concern for her family, but avoid expressing gratitude for his service to the country. Queen Victoria's refusal to thank him for his service haunted Gladstone for the rest of his life. Those who knew Gladstone respected him for his desire for peace, his trust in the masses, and his zeal in the cause of freedom.

A year before she died, Victoria would take a spring vacation in Ireland. From the moment of her arrival in the port of Kingstown, she wore shamrocks (the national emblem of Ireland) pinned to her dresses and carried a parasol decorated with the insignia. The eighty-one-year-old queen needed a wheelchair to get around because of her painful rheumatism, and she sometimes dozed at receptions. Although her visit was well intentioned, it could not make up for years of neglect. Anti-British feelings were growing stronger, and the independence Gladstone had advocated would not be accomplished until a long period filled with terrorism and bloodshed had passed.

By the end of the nineteenth century, Great Britain's imperial possessions were the envy of the western world. The poet Rudyard Kipling famously said that the sun never set on the British Empire, stretching as it did all over the world. Many English emigrated to the colonies because they had good weather and abundant natural resources. There was also the chance to make a great fortune and to have a better life away from the industrial slums of England. These

The British Empire (marked in red) in 1895. *(National Maritime Museum, London.)*

colonists, however, often discovered that the British government was much more repressive in the colonies than it was back home. British citizens abroad often became the loudest advocates for self-government of the colonies. The British government's main concern was keeping the valuable natural resources flowing from the colonies to England. British steel mills needed iron and other minerals, and the vast English textile industry depended on Egyptian and Indian cotton and dyes. As long as the colonial rulers maintained this economic connection, the British were usually willing to loosen political control.

During the last decades of Victoria's reign, the government began to encourage limited democratic self-government in several British colonies, including Canada, Australia, New Zealand, and the Cape Colony in South Africa. The American Revolution had taught Britain that it would be wiser to allow their colonial possessions some measure of freedom than to lose them completely.

Gradually, Britain transformed itself from an empire to a commonwealth. The term "commonwealth" first came into use in the 1860s to describe the new relationship between Britain and Canada, which was given dominion status in 1867. Australia received dominion status in 1900, New Zealand in 1907, and South Africa in 1910. Becoming a dominion meant the country was self-governing, but remained sworn in symbolic loyalty to the British crown and, most importantly, would give the British favorable trade agreements. This arrangement relieved the British government of the expense of administering and maintaining a military force in the far-away nations, while enabling it to enjoy trade advantages over the rest of Europe and the United States.

Along with witnessing the transfiguration of the British empire, Victoria's reign saw incredible advances in technology, many of which helped to make the world a little smaller. Railroads and cheap postage meant letters went farther, faster. The electric telegraph connected Britain to far-off India by 1878, and ten years later, in Great Britain alone, there were 26,000 of Alexander Graham Bell's new telephones. The world was a rapidly changing place.

Conflicts at Home and Abroad

As she aged, Victoria was slow to embrace the changes going on around her. Because she spent so much time at Balmoral and avoided attending as many public events as possible, many felt she was neglecting her duties more than ever. A cartoon of the time portrayed an empty throne and the caption "Where is Britannia?" The queen was undeterred by the criticism and peevish with those who urged her to return to public life. She complained constantly about her health and argued that, given her age and other woes, she was doing all that she could.

Queen Victoria was not always beloved by her people. Her stubbornness made her seem haughty at times, but other times it was taken for bravery—as when she had refused protective measures after assassination attempts. Albert's death brought the queen the country's sympathy, but her extended mourning seemed self-indulgent. Then, in 1870, international affairs caused her popularity to drop again.

WHERE IS BRITANNIA ?

Prussian leader Otto von Bismarck had long hoped to unite the German states under his command. A crafty politician, he goaded France into declaring war in order to bond the German states together against a common enemy.

Victoria's oldest daughter and favorite child, Vicky, was married to Prince Friedrich of Prussia, the heir to the Prussian throne. A Germany unified under Prussian leadership had been a long-time dream of Prince Albert. Victoria needed to appear publicly neutral about the conflict but privately she deplored "the *extreme iniquity* of the war, and the unjustifiable conduct of the French." The war was over quickly and Napoleon III surrendered on September 2, 1870. Victoria did what she could to comfort his wife, Eugénie, who sought sanctuary in England.

Bismarck's plan to use the war to unify the German states worked. However, the fall of the emperor led to the creation of a republic in France. There would be no more French kings or emperors. Supporters of a republic in Great Britain became openly hostile toward Victoria as they watched the French crown being abolished. She attacked those who disputed the supreme power of the throne: "she [the queen] *cannot* and will not be the Queen of a *democratic monarchy*; and those who have spoken and agitated . . . must look for *another monarch;* and she doubts they will find one."

One of the major criticisms the republicans levied against the monarchy was its cost. Victoria and her households were a financial drain on the country. Each of her adult children was granted an annuity by Parliament. These yearly amounts were usually around twenty thousand pounds. The princesses were given an additional sum for their dowries. In an era when a laborer earned only about fifty pounds a year and a skilled engineer could earn less than a hundred, the royal family consumed a disproportionate amount of money. A pamphlet entitled *What Does She Do With It?* criticized Victoria's annual income and wondered if the country received any gain from having a queen. But when she appeared in public after a month of isolation, even her opponents had to admit she did not look well. She had lost nearly thirty pounds and looked pale and drawn. Gladstone came to her aid and stopped a bill in Parliament ordering an investigation of her financial status.

As had happened decades earlier, another assassination attempt restored the queen's popularity. She was riding in a carriage one day in 1872 when a deranged man ran toward her waving a pistol. John Brown grabbed the attacker and wrestled him to the ground, thereby earning public acclaim as a hero. Though it was later determined that he did not mean to harm the queen, only to scare her into signing a petition he had, the man was publicly decried as a criminal. The incident helped John Brown's reputation as well. The insinuations about his close relationship with the queen began to die down; many now saw him as a loyal protector and friend.

Victoria's family gave her little comfort. She was a controlling and perpetually disappointed parent, always warning her children not to put their hands in their pockets, not to smoke, hunt, or go yachting, which she banned because, she said, the others involved in the sport were "the very worst people." She complained about the way her children raised their own children. Their social lives were filled with too many parties and too much frivolity. Always,

The royal Family at Osborne House in 1870: Princess Beatrice, Prince Leopold, the queen, Princess Louise, Princess Alexandra, and several of Victoria's grandchildren.

it was Bertie, the unworthy namesake of her departed husband, who worried her most of all. His gambling and adultery was an almost constant source of scandal. It was speculated that the aging queen, who expressed no pleasure in her duties as monarch, would consider stepping down if she had a more suitable heir. But Victoria could not entertain such thoughts as long as Bertie was next in line.

In the fall of 1871 Bertie came down with typhoid, the same disease that killed his father. He was near death for several days. Once he had regained his strength, the queen faced the problem of what to do with him. Gladstone had suggested that she establish a residence in Ireland to show her concern for the people there, but she refused. Next, Gladstone suggested they appoint Bertie viceroy of Ireland, but she declined this idea also, concerned about letting the irresponsible prince out of her sight. He was not fit for the army, and showed no interest in anything but horse racing, hunting, and women. The queen wrote often to her daughters about how sad it made her that her heir was so worthless. The queen suffered a series of illnesses herself in 1871, including an inflamed throat, an abscess on her arm, gout, and rheumatism.

In 1874, some good news came when Gladstone was voted out of office. Victoria was delighted to receive the seventy-year-old Disraeli again as prime minister. He and Victoria saw eye-to-eye on the need to strengthen and extend the British Empire. Unlike Gladstone, Disraeli never scolded or talked down to her. He explained how he got along so well with her: "I never refuse; I never contradict;

I sometimes forget." He told a friend, "You have heard me called a flatterer, and it is true. Everyone likes flattery; and when you come to royalty, you would lay it on with a trowel." Unlike Gladstone, Disraeli kept Victoria informed about government business and discussed with her the reactions of Parliament.

Disraeli reached the zenith of his political influence from 1874 to 1876. During these months Parliament, under his guidance, passed six major bills intended to improve the lives of the British people. The bills expanded the vote to more of the working class, improved the legal standing of tenant farmers, protected women and children who worked in factories, improved housing and working conditions for the poor, and offered better safety and protection to the consumers of food and drugs. These were highly popular bills that attracted working class voters to the Conservative (Tory) Party. Victoria assented to Disraeli's combination of domestic political reforms and more aggressive policies abroad.

One of Disraeli's central foreign policy concerns was the Suez Canal. Opened by the French in 1869, the one-hundred-and-one-mile-long canal cut across northeastern Egypt to connect the Red Sea to the Mediterranean. Now ships could get to India from Britain without having to go around the huge landmass of Africa. When the canal first opened, three-quarters of the ships passing through were British, and it soon became essential to British commerce. The canal was strategically important to the British navy, as well.

In 1875, Egypt was struggling beneath a heavy debt.

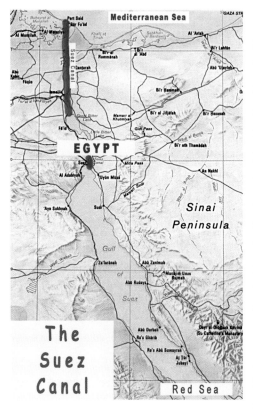

The
Suez
Canal

Seeing an opportunity, Disraeli outbid the French and acquired the Egyptian shares of the canal for Britain for four million pounds. Gladstone and his supporters in the Liberal Party criticized the purchase as a foolish waste of money. Victoria stood firmly behind Disraeli.

The Suez Canal gave Britain significant control over an important—and much shorter—route to India. Victoria decided the time was right for her to accept the title of empress of India. After a long, bitter fight in Parliament, the title was granted to her in 1876. Those opposed to the title, led again by Gladstone, argued that being queen of England was the highest honor in the world. She should not feel the need to complement that honor with any other. Others warned, presciently, that by publicly claiming India, the monarchy would be that much more insulted if it was ever lost. Victoria ignored these grumblings and from that time on happily signed herself Victoria R & I which stood for *Regina et Imperatrix*

"NEW CROWNS FOR OLD ONES!"

This contemporary caricature shows an obsequious Benjamin Disraeli presenting Victoria with the crown of India in exchange for the British crown.

(queen and empress).

Gladstone and Disraeli clashed again over foreign policy as tensions between Russia and Turkey resurfaced. Twenty years before, Britain had fought the bloody Crimean War to try to contain Russian aggression against Turkey. Now Russia was stirring up trouble again, this time supporting rebels inside Turkey who were fighting the Ottoman rulers. Turkey had become increasingly unstable since the Crimean War, and during the 1870s, Russia encouraged several nationalistic and ethnic groups to rise up in revolt. The Turks attempted to squelch these movements, killing more than ten thousand rebels in the process. Most of Europe condemned the Turkish atrocities.

Gladstone was particularly moved by the massacres, and even produced a pamphlet on the subject. He was appalled by the Turkish government's use of what he considered to be unnecessary force. When it appeared that Russia might be ready to openly attack Turkey, Gladstone urged British neutrality, feeling the British government should not support the despotic and murderous Turks even if Russia did invade. Disraeli, on the other hand, dismissed the reports of Turkish atrocities as exaggerations. He, like Victoria, thought a powerful Russia was more dangerous than a disorganized and internally divided Turkey. Most of the British public sided with him, trained as they were to fear Russia.

The Russians declared war on Turkey in 1877. Victoria urged that Britons stand firmly behind the Turks, but Parliament was divided between Disraeli and Gladstone, and no decision could be made on either side. Frustrated that Parliament could not come to a consensus about the war, Victoria wrote, "If the Queen were a man, she would like to go and give those Russians, whose word one cannot believe, such a beating!"

While the world watched, the Russians quickly defeated the Turks and moved in to take over Constantinople, the capital of Turkey, as well as some ports on the Aegean Sea. Victoria complained that Great Britain should have sent troops to Constantinople to stop the Russians. She wrote a letter to one of her daughters: "I never saw anything to equal the want of patriotism and the want of proper decency in Members of Parliament. It is a miserable thing to be a constitutional Queen, and to be unable to do what is right. I would gladly throw all up and retire into quiet." She wrote to Disraeli, "If England is to kiss Russia's feet, she [the queen] will not be a party to the humiliation of England and would lay down her crown."

Victoria's fears were given new credence when the terms

of the peace treaty were announced. They were hugely favorable to Russia. Confident of getting support from most of the rest of Europe, Russia called for a congress in Berlin to ratify the terms of the agreement. Most British citizens shared Victoria's conviction that Russia must be thwarted at the negotiation table.

In the spring of 1878, though he was seventy-four years old and in poor health, Victoria appointed Disraeli as special ambassador to the peace conference in Berlin. He went with two goals: to protect the weakened Turkey and to protect British access to sea routes to Asia. Although he was forced to grant the Russians more Turkish territory than he wanted, he did secure for the British possession of Cyprus, an island in the Mediterranean Sea off the southern coast of Turkey. This gave the British fleet a base from which Disraeli promised to defend Turkey from future Russian aggression. Returning to Britain a hero, Disraeli had won what he called "peace with honor."

Disraeli's imperialist policies continued to put him at odds with Gladstone. Disraeli worried that Russia would invade Afghanistan and threaten the British control of India. He acted aggressively to try to contain Russia. During his second term as prime minister, Disraeli sent troops into Afghanistan and present-day Pakistan to create a buffer zone between Russia and India. Disraeli also committed troops to what became known as the Zulu War in Africa.

Many European nations, including Great Britain, coveted the natural resources and fertile farmland of Africa. From 1820 on, British settlers spread across the southern part of the continent. The indigenous Zulus fought to defend their land from invasion. They inflicted stinging defeats on the British during much of 1878 but, by 1879, had succumbed to superior forces. In a few years, Great Britain would be engaged in an even bloodier conflict brought on by its reach into southern Africa.

Gladstone spoke out against Disraeli's use of British troops in Africa, the annexation of Cyprus, the conflicts in Afghanistan and Egypt, and the ongoing troubles in Ireland and India. He argued that the Conservatives, allied with the queen, were intent only on glorifying themselves by expanding British territory. He attacked what he called imperialist wars and even attacked Queen Victoria herself as an imperialist. Great Britain should not pursue such policies, he said, but should be a cooperative country working toward peace everywhere.

Victoria never understood Gladstone's position. She believed the best way to prevent future violence was to station heavily armed troops in troubled areas. The presence of these troops would stop the violence before it happened and make the world safer: "The *true economy is to be always ready. It will prevent war,*" she said. Frustrated that Gladstone would not agree, Victoria wrote to Disraeli: "We must, with our Indian Empire and large colonies, be prepared for attacks and wars, somewhere or other, continually."

Gladstone was not popular with his fellow politicians, but he was well liked by most citizens. In a general election in 1880, the Liberals achieved a landslide victory. Victoria was very disappointed to lose the devoted and obliging

Disraeli. She was determined to stop Gladstone from becoming prime minister in his place. She declared that he never was, and never could be, loyal to the queen. Although his Liberals had won 349 seats compared to the Tory's 243, she said she would "sooner abdicate than send for or have any communication with that half-mad firebrand who would soon ruin everything and be a Dictator."

Victoria's antagonism toward Gladstone changed nothing. She was compelled by the constitution to accept him as prime minister. She could only watch helplessly as he pulled British troops out of Afghanistan.

Between 1880 and 1885 Gladstone wrote more than a thousand letters to Victoria, all in his own hand, all based on careful research. Nevertheless, the queen complained that Gladstone shut her out of important decisions, saying "I am so overdone, so vexed, and in such distress about my country . . . I will daily pray for God's help to improve." For his part, Gladstone felt he was going overboard to pacify an intrusive sovereign. Though she wrote to him constantly, the few times they met in person Victoria steered the conversation to unimportant topics, such as the weather and the health of mutual friends. She could not bring herself to speak of politics to the man she so despised. Gladstone was heard to say, "the queen alone is enough to kill any man."

The queen took comfort in her continued close relationship with Disraeli. When he died, just a year after leaving office, Victoria was deeply moved by his passing and felt, once again, that she had been left alone in the world.

Gladstone's time in power did not bring peace to Britain's

The situation in Egypt and Sudan continued to worsen as Victoria and Gladstone argued about how to best resolve it. After several instances where Imperial troops were overpowered in Africa, the Britsh decided to respond. This battle in Sudan pitted an army of desert tribesmen against the full British military force and resulted in a bloody defeat of the Sudanese.

enormous empire. Soon after he took office, a revolt in Egypt threatened British control of the Suez Canal. Because the British were so heavily invested in India, they could not tolerate losing control of the canal. Gladstone had no choice but to send in troops. While peace was restored to the canal area, British troops there suddenly faced attacks from rebels based in Sudan, just south of Egypt.

As Gladstone debated the wisdom of sending British troops into Sudan, Victoria pressured him to do so. "We must not retire [from Egypt] without making our power felt," she insisted. Victoria was, as usual, in favor of a strong international presence, but Gladstone, as usual, did not agree. The situation worsened as Gladstone considered his options.

As the European countries began jockeying to claim territory in Africa, German chancellor Otto von Bismarck called the Congress of Berlin to discuss general ground rules for the European division of the continent—ignoring completely the rights of the people already living there. The most important principle established was that a territory had to be occupied in order for a country to claim it. This set off the "Scramble for Africa" as European nations hurried to lay claim to territory, hoping to secure profitable colonies.

Gladstone remained reluctant to increase Britain's international presence, but after the Congress of Berlin he realized that if England did not make a stand, it would lose out in Africa. In January 1885, Gladstone sent troops to Egypt—but it was too late. Thousands of British soldiers died before the armed conflict ended with a victory for the rebels. Victoria was furious and declared that Gladstone was "responsible by imprudence and neglect, for the lives of many thousands." Gladstone was so angry when he learned of this comment that he vowed never again to set foot in Windsor Castle.

In June 1885, the Liberals lost to the Tories by twelve

votes. Gladstone immediately resigned, saying that he would never again stand for a general election. Victoria was in Scotland at the time and refused to return to London to preside over the change in power as her royal duties dictated. She complained that she was nearing seventy years old (she was sixty-six) and could not move from place to place as easily as she used to. She asked the Conservative leader, Lord Salisbury, to form a new government. She believed he would protect and extend British interests throughout the world. Salisbury accepted the queen's offer and became prime minister, but he lasted just over six months. After losing a confidence vote, Salisbury resigned, and despite his earlier promise to the contrary, Gladstone returned to office. Six months later, after losing the battle over Home Rule, he was gone again—this time, for good. Victoria would see Gladstone just a few more times before he died. He remained bitter until the end at her refusal to thank him for his services to the country.

Salisbury returned to office and served from 1886-1892. He tried to replace Disraeli in the queen's affections and worked to expand the British Empire. He secured possession of Northern and Southern Rhodesia (now Zambia and Zimbabwe) and part of East Africa. He also saw Parliament pass the Third Reform Bill, in 1888, which gave the vote to about 2,000,000 rural workers.

Salisbury was also in office at the time of the Boer War, from 1899-1902. In the fall of 1899 the Boers—Dutch colonists in South Africa—took up arms against British settlers who had demanded control of the extensive mineral wealth they had developed. The Dutch had been in South Africa since the seventeenth century; the British had only become a force in the nineteenth century. One constant point of contention was the way the Boers treated the African people, who lived as virtual slaves. The Boers made efforts to expand their territory further north, but over the years the British established states on both sides of the Boers. Even-

Lord Salisbury.

tually, the British government began to send in settlers to Dutch areas and insisted they be given the right to vote. When the Boers refused, saying the English settlers could not vote until they had been residents of the Boer states for seven years, Great Britain sent in 70,000 soldiers to seize all of South Africa. Fierce and bloody fighting ensued.

This time, Victoria's contributions to the war effort were not political. She read the newspaper reports avidly and encouraged soldiers in letters and public statements of praise. She even joined in the effort to knit scarves and comforters for them; each soldier receiving one could imagine his had been knitted by the queen. For Christmas 1901, she sent 100,000 tins of chocolate to front-line troops. The tins were embossed with her picture and were highly valued by the soldiers. There were reports that several even stopped bullets, saving the lives of those who carried them.

The war was terrible, but by July, Britain had successfully annexed the republics of Transvaal and Orange Free State. After eighteen more months of fighting, the Boers, unhappily, became British subjects. Victoria's reign had seen another expansion of the British Empire.

12

"I Will Be Good"

The grand Colonial and Indian Exhibition of 1886 re-minded Victoria of Albert's Great Exhibition. Like the original, this exhibition was designed to showcase England's power to the world—this time, through flaunting the wealth and culture of its colonies. Victoria attended proudly. She carried with her at all times a locket with Albert's picture engraved in it, and at the exhibition she could be seen holding it aloft in order to "show" Albert the things he had not seen during his lifetime.

In June 1887, Victoria celebrated her Golden Jubilee, the fiftieth anniversary of her ascension to the throne. She finally agreed to drive through the streets in a carriage, but she refused to wear a crown or royal robe. She had worn nothing but black since Albert's death, and she would not change. Her only concession was to load herself with jewels and don a cap of white lace decorated with feathers. At 11:30 on the morning of June 21, she set out to retrace her journey from Buckingham Palace to Westminster Abbey. She sat in an open carriage while her children and grandchildren headed the procession. Thousands of people gathered on sidewalks, at open widows, and on rooftops to cheer. She received guests at lunch, dinner, and a reception before slipping away to her room, as the music of "Rule, Britannia" was played on the mall.

Victoria's Jubilee celebration capped her transition from an influential political figure to a figurehead queen. Many of Victoria's subjects had never known another ruler and did not remember the days when the monarch was an important part of the government. The queen was a just tiny old woman dressed in black—yet she was also a symbol of the longevity and stability of the British empire.

One member of the House of Lords captured that sentiment when he described his impression of the Jubilee celebrations in a letter to the queen: "All was worthy of your Majesty and of the Empire; all has tended to strengthen and to deepen the foundations of a monarchy which overshadows the globe, and represents the union and aspirations of three hundred millions of human beings."

Victoria was deeply touched by her Golden Jubilee. She wrote to an aide: "It is impossible for me to say how deeply, immensely touched and gratified I have been and am by the wonderful and so universal enthusiasm displayed by my people, by high and low, rich and poor . . . as well as the respect shown by foreign rulers and their peoples. . . . It

Throughout the country, streets were lined with decorations for Victoria's Jubilee procession. This scene shows the festivities in one of London's liveliest areas, Picadilly Circus.

shows that fifty years' hard work, anxiety, and care have been appreciated, and that my sympathy with the sorrowing, suffering, and humble is acknowledged."

As she neared the end of her long life, Victoria's attitudes towards her subjects continued to evolve. She took up the cause of the poor who lived in overcrowded and unsanitary homes and suffered from the lack of nutrition, medicine, and sanitation. She was pleased to see a welfare reform bill passed that took some steps to improve their situation.

She was still unhappy at the prospect of Bertie assuming

the throne. Though by now well into middle age, Bertie had done little to convince her that he was prepared to rule. He was chronically in debt from his life of women and gambling. There seemed to be no end to the stories of scandal connected to him. The *Pall Mall Gazette* printed an editorial about the monarchy asking, "How long will it last we wonder. . . . As long as the Queen lasts, yes, but after the Queen, who knows?" The queen had no way of knowing that when Bertie did ascend to the throne to become Edward VII, he would throw himself into the role of king with marked vitality until his death in 1910.

As she entered her eighties, the short, heavyset queen began to have trouble getting around. She spent most of her waking hours in a wheelchair at Balmoral, where some of her notorious frugality was observed by visitors shocked to discover that the queen provided only squares of old newspaper for toilet paper. Though she preferred to be alone, Victoria kept up with the news from London. She took an interest in the stories of the murderous Jack the Ripper, who attacked and killed prostitutes in London's slums. Victoria sent several letters to Parliament with suggestions as to how detectives might find the killer. Despite her efforts, he was never caught. She further occupied her time by studying Hindi with an Indian secretary, Abdul Karim.

As Victoria neared her eightieth birthday, in 1897, her health continued to decline. She suffered from cataracts that left her nearly blind. She traveled when she could, but needed an entourage of nearly one hundred attendants and her own bed. She made it a point to visit wounded soldiers at every opportunity. In each ward, Victoria was wheeled up and down the aisles, stopping to offer a word of thanks to each invalid. She took real pleasure in seeing performances of all the latest plays and other theatrical entertainment.

Victoria continued to entertain, and her dinners were always elaborate and predictable. She greeted each guest individually with a formal politeness, engaged in a bit of stiff dialogue, and then went on to the next guest while the others watched in silence. Such formality became one of the symbols of what was called the Victorian Age. Operas and plays were less formal occasions, during which the queen allowed herself to participate in the drama or humor or pathos of the stories unfolding before her. She retained a sense of humor and laughed heartily at comedies.

One story about her was of her meeting with Admiral Seymour whose ship, the *Sea Mew,* had recently capsized. Victoria asked about the health of the admiral's wife. Hard of hearing, he thought she had asked about his ship. He answered "All right, thank you, Ma'am. We've got her on her side, and tomorrow we are going to scrape her bottom." There was a breathless pause while her attendants looked on, stricken, until the queen laughed heartily at the mistake.

Victoria became increasingly stubborn as she grew older. Sir Henry Ponsonby, her private secretary, explained how he worked with her: "When she insists that two and two make five I say that I cannot help thinking that they make four. She replies that there may be some truth in what I say, but she knows they make five. Thereupon I drop the discussion."

On September 23, 1896, Victoria wrote proudly, "Today is the day on which I have reigned longer, by a day, than any English sovereign." She would make her Diamond Jubilee, celebrating her sixtieth year as queen, a celebration of the British Empire and an affirmation of all Great Britain had achieved in her name. The honored guests were representatives of the Empire: prime ministers of the dominions and colonies, Indian princes, African chiefs, dignitaries from Hong Kong and the Pacific islands. An elaborate pageant presented the assembled people of different races joining the "family" of the British crown. Soldiers from India, Australia, Borneo, Cyprus, South Africa, and Hong Kong paraded through the streets in a mighty show of the expansive British Empire. The latest innovation in technology allowed her to send a cable to all parts of the Empire: "From my heart I thank my beloved people. May God bless them!" She wrote in her journal: "The streets, the windows, the roofs of the houses, were one mass of beaming faces, and the cheers never ceased."

As the years passed, the queen's eyesight continued to worsen. First she could hardly read, and gradually even signing her name became difficult. Her memory failed her more and more often. About her physical appearance, she told her daughter "God knows there is nothing to admire in my ugly old person."

As 1900 became 1901, Victoria wrote in her diary: "Another year begun and I am feeling so weak and unwell that I enter upon it sadly." She did take regular drives in a carriage with her ladies or rode in a small cart pulled by a

Victoria on a carriage ride near the time of her Diamond Jubilee. *(Courtesy of Getty Images.)*

donkey. These rides became a project for Victoria's servants since she took along a collection of rugs, parasols, and drawing materials. She was lifted into the carriage from a set of carpeted steps.

Throughout January, the queen slept more and more each day and appeared dazed when she finally awoke. Her left cheek drooped and she spoke with some impediment, perhaps due to an undiagnosed stroke. The doctor confirmed the opinion of those close to her that her mind was rapidly failing. Her family was alerted but told that a public statement should not be made for fear of creating alarm. At one point she told her doctor that she wanted to live a little longer because she had business to settle. Once she sat up and cried out, "Oh, Albert," then sank onto the pillow again. Queen Victoria died at 6:30 P.M. on January 22, 1901, surrounded by many of her children, grandchildren, and thirty-seven great-grandchildren.

Newspapers all over the world expressed universal grief and acknowledged the passing of an age. The streets of London were quiet except for the tolling of the great bell of Christ Church. Victoria had left detailed instructions for her military funeral. She asked to be buried in white because at her death she would join Albert and would no longer need widow's clothes. Following her instructions, her family placed mementos in her coffin: Albert's dressing gown, a plaster cast of his hand, and a number of family photographs. Her coffin was put on the yacht *Alberta,* which cruised in Portsmouth Harbor while long lines of warships thundered their salutes. The coffin was then put on a train to Paddington Station. Mourners were allowed to kneel along the track to pay their respects. Then it was placed in a gun carriage and driven to the Albert Memorial Chapel in London where officers stood silent and motionless guard during a memorial service. Victoria's final journey was to the mausoleum where her beloved Albert was buried.

Victoria's funeral procession from the Albert Memorial Chapel to the Frogmore Mausoleum at Windsor Castle on February 4, 1901.

Queen Victoria reigned for sixty-three years. In the nineteenth century, the average life expectancy in Great Britain was less than sixty years, which means thousands of her subjects lived their entire life knowing only one monarch. Her name was given to one of the most clearly defined periods in European history.

During Victoria's reign, Great Britain was transformed from a mostly agricultural country with an isolationist foreign policy to a dominant industrial and military power. By 1901, the year of her death, the sun truly never set on the British Empire. Vast holdings in India, the Middle East, and Africa assured a steady supply of raw materials to British factories. English merchants traveled the globe selling products and purchasing exotic goods that could be sold to the newly wealthy middle class at home. Victoria was the first British monarch to ride a train; when she died, the age of the automobile was dawning. Charles Dickens, Alfred Tennyson, George Bernard Shaw, Thomas Hardy, Rudyard Kipling, and George Eliot are only a few of the British writers who flourished during her years on the throne. London became a center of painting, theater, and music, all of which depended on the wealth that flowed from the expanding commerce and production she oversaw.

The years of Victoria's reign were also years of political and economic reform. When she assumed power, the landless and often wageless workers who had flooded the cities could not vote. Parliament was filled with members of the old landed aristocracy who had gerrymandered the electoral districts to assure that only their interests would receive attention. There was no social safety net for the poor, the unskilled, and the uneducated. To be in poverty in London, Birmingham, Manchester, and other cities meant living on the street, begging, and stealing food. Without the power to vote, those British citizens left out of the new economy of the nineteenth century had little hope of improving their lives.

Out of this despair there slowly emerged one of the first successful reform movements in history. Other European countries with similar problems, such as France, went through a series of political revolts and coups that changed not only leaders but how the government was structured. Great Britain went through the turmoil of the Chartist movement, the Anti-Corn Law League, and other reform movements, during which prime ministers lost their jobs and parties collapsed, but the monarchy and the British political infrastructure remained intact.

Throughout these years of rapid change, reform, reaction, and growing imperialistic power, Queen Victoria presented a complex public image. Although she was known for her frugality, she always traveled with a large staff of servants and ate off plates of solid gold, her hands so weighted with jewels it was said she had trouble lifting a knife and fork. Despite the widely held assumption that the natives of distant and recently subjugated areas were barbarians, she remained remarkably free of religious prejudice. A strong, even domineering, woman who held her own with powerful male politicians and advisors, she considered the idea of women's suffrage to be "mad, wicked folly." She was sure that women would become troublesome, and even hateful, if allowed equal rights with men. She pushed her prime ministers to expand the empire and to send troops into battle, then wept over the casualty reports.

Victoria came to embody the virtues of her time: industry, responsibility, devotion to family, and honesty; as well as inflexibility, prudery, and strict attention to the rules of decorum.

During Victoria's reign, the political power of the crown continued its inevitable decline. She began her reign as part of a constitutional monarchy and by the time of her death the monarchy was almost purely symbolic. As British power expanded, her own power shrank. But she relished her symbolic role and remained determined to be the first Hanoverian to increase—not diminish—the crown's prestige.

Victoria ensured the survival of the monarchy in England while other European kings and queens were being tossed into the dustbin of history. It is more than a little ironic that the most modern and highly developed nation in Europe was also the one that best accommodated this prominent symbol of the past. By the end of the century, there was no longer a royal family in France, and the German royal family would end with the defeat of Victoria's grandson's forces in World War I. Queen Victoria presided over the development of a robust and thriving democracy in Great Britain. She appealed to her subjects as both an ordinary person who sympathized with their joys and sorrows and as a dignified tribute to their national history. Honest, patriotic, and determined, Victoria succeeded, in her own way, in fulfilling her childhood promise to always "be good" when she became the queen of her beloved country. Her death was truly the end of an era.

Timeline

1819   Victoria is born on May 24.

1837   Queen Victoria comes to the throne.

1840   Marriage of Queen Victoria to Prince Albert.

1842   Opening of the Great Western railway.

1845   Potato famine hits Ireland.

1846   Corn Laws are abolished.

1848   Revolutions break out in a number of Western and Central European countries.

1850   The first public libraries open.

1851   Great Exhibition opens in Crystal Palace.

1854   The Crimean War begins, lasting through 1856.

1856   Victoria Cross is created to reward bravery in battle.

1857   The Indian Mutiny erupts, continuing into 1858.

1861   Prince Albert dies from typhoid; the American Civil War begins.

1867   The second Reform Act is passed.

1869   The Suez Canal is opened in Egypt.

1876   First telephone call made by Alexander Graham Bell.

1877   Queen Victoria made empress of India.

1879   The Anglo-Zulu War takes place in South Africa; Britain invades Afghanistan.

1880   The first Boer War.

1881   Boers defeat British in Boer War.

1884   Third Reform Act passed by Parliament; through 1885, the Berlin Conference sets off the "Scramble for Africa."

1888   Jack the Ripper terrorizes London.

1896   The British invade Sudan.

1897   Queen Victoria's Jubliee.

1899   The second Boer War.

1901   On January 22, Queen Victoria dies.

QUEEN VICTORIA'S PRIME MINISTERS:

1837-1841   William Lamb (Lord Melbourne)

1841-1846   Robert Peel

1846–1852   John Russell

1852-1855   George Hamilton (Earl of Aberdeen)

1855-1858   Henry John Temple (Lord Palmerston)

1858-1859   Edward Geoffrey Smith Stanley (Earl of Derby)

1859-1865   Lord Palmerston

1865-1866   Sir John Russell

1866-1868   Earl of Derby

1868   Benjamin Disraeli

1868-1874   William Gladstone

1874-188   Benjamin Disraeli

1880-1885   William Gladstone

1885-1886   Robert Arthur Gascoyne-Cecil (Lord Salisbury)

1886   William Gladstone

1886-1892   Lord Salisbury

1892-1894   William Gladstone

1894-1895   Archibald Philip Primrose (Earl of Rosebery)

1895-1901   Lord Salisbury

Sources

CHAPTER ONE: The New Queen

p. 13, "I am very young and . . ." Christopher Hibbert, ed., *Queen Victoria in Her Letters and Journals* (New York: Viking, 1985), 27.

p. 14, "Let me be by . . ." Lytton Strachey, *Queen Victoria* (New York: Harcourt, Brace & World, Inc., 1921), 40.

p. 14, "You do not know . . ." Cecil Woodham-Smith, *Queen Victoria: From Her Birth to the Death of the Prince Consort* (New York: Alfred A. Knopf, 1972),142.

p. 18, "be good" Giles St. Aubyn, *Queen Victoria: A Portrait* (New York: Atheneum, 1992), 25.

CHAPTER TWO: An Uncertain Childhood

p. 21, "Take care of her . . ." St. Aubyn, *Queen Victoria*, 9.

p. 26, "Two storms . . ." Elizabeth Longford, *Queen Victoria: Born to Succeed* (New York: Harper & Row, Publishers, 1964), 28.

p. 26, "No, Mama . . ." Ibid.

p. 26, "There, now . . ." Ibid., 31.

p. 27, "a great blessing . . ." St. Aubyn, *Queen Victoria*, 17.

p. 28, "I see I am nearer . . ." Longford, *Queen Victoria*, 32.

p. 28, "I will be good." St. Aubyn, *Queen Victoria*, 25.

p. 29, "I am today . . ." Hibbert, 12.

p. 29, "You are now fourteen . . ." St. Aubyn, 35.

p. 29, "to act with great impartiality . . ." Strachey, 36.

p. 29, "I look up to him . . ." St. Aubyn, 35.

p. 30, "I resisted in spite . . ." Ibid, 38.

p. 31, "How far I am . . ." Hibbert, 21.

CHAPTER THREE: Coronation

p. 32, "I hope royal authority . . ." Longford, *Queen Victoria*, 54.

p. 37, "I felt for the first . . ." Hibbert, *Queen Victoria*, 27.

p. 38, "The Country continues . . ." St. Aubyn, *Queen Victoria*, 31.

p. 39, "I don't *like* those . . . leave them alone." Ibid., 82.

p. 41, "I received so . . ." Longford, *Queen Victoria*, 74.

p. 42, "she laughs in real earnest . . ." Dorothy Thompson, *Queen Victoria: The Woman, The Monarch, and The People* (New York: Pantheon Books, 1990), 44.

p. 43, "Very well, my . . ." Longford, *Queen Victoria*, 76.

p. 43, "Upon this one subject . . ." Strachey, 108.

p. 46, "good humor and excessive loyalty . . ." Gernsheim, Helmut and Alison, *Victoria R.* (New York: G. P. Putnam's Sons, 1959), 16.

CHAPTER FOUR: A Royal Wedding

p. 50, "it was 10 to 1 . . ." St. Aubyn, *Queen Victoria*, 126.

p. 51, "Albert really is quite . . ." Woodham-Smith, *Queen Victoria*, 183.

p. 51, "has a beautiful . . ." Hibbert, *Queen Victoria*, 17.

p. 52, "made a very favorable . . ." Woodham-Smith, *Queen Victoria*, 183.

p. 53, "it would make me . . ." Strachey, *Queen Victoria*, 71.

p. 53, "V. is said to be . . ." Gernsheim, *Victoria R.*, 14.

p. 53, "using his powers and . . ." Ibid., 16.

p. 53, "I intend to train . . ." Longford, *Queen Victoria*, 130.

p. 54, "I feel the happiest . . ." Hibbert, *Queen Victoria*, 57.

p. 54, "Come to take . . ." Thompson, *Queen Victoria*, 34.

p. 54, "I have always had . . ." Gernsheim, *Victoria R.*,14.

p. 54, "though not as a *queen* . . ." Ibid., 38.

p. 55, "abominable, infamous " St. Aubyn, *Queen Victoria*, 140.

p. 56, "You forget, my dearest . . ." Woodham-Smith, *Queen Victoria*, 206.

CHAPTER FIVE: Family and Home

p. 61, "There is often an irritability . . ." Hibbert, *Queen Victoria*, 94.

p. 61, "How uncontrollable my . . ." St. Aubyn, *Queen Victoria*, 167.

p. 62, "Walked with my ANGELIC . . ." Longford, *Queen Victoria*, 86.

p. 63, "A requisition is . . ." St. Aubyn, *Queen Victoria*, 179.

p. 64, "Who is there . . . Your wife." Gernsheim, *Victoria R.*, 40.

p. 65, "a perfect little . . ." St. Aubyn, *Queen Victoria*, 165.

p. 66, "I have no tender [tenderness] . . ." Ibid., 167.

p. 67, "I cannot forebear . . ." Strachey, *Queen Victoria*, 171.

p. 68, "Poor Bertie! He vexes us . . ." Hibbert, *Queen Victoria*, 107.

CHAPTER SIX: Ireland

p. 72, "I cannot bear to . . ." St. Aubyn, *Queen Victoria*, 311.

p. 73, "To hear of their [the poor] . . ." Ibid., 263.

p. 77, "but a faint impression . . ." Ibid., 117.

p. 78, "Really, they [the rebels] . . ." Longford, *Queen Victoria*, 198.

p. 78, "Obedience to the laws & to the . . ." Ibid.

CHAPTER SEVEN: Great Exhibition

p. 80, "the *greatest* day . . ." Strachey, *Queen Victoria*, 101.

p. 81, "Now this monstrous . . ." Thompson, *Queen Victoria*, 119.

CHAPTER EIGHT: Pax Britannica

p. 91, "One man who had . . ." Hibbert, *Queen Victoria*, 130.

p. 95, "too horrible and . . ." St. Aubyn, *Queen Victoria*, 306.

p. 96, "that there is no . . ." Gernsheim, *Victoria R.*, 61.

p. 96, "India shd [should] belong to me." Longford, *Queen Victoria*, 280.

p. 96, "with every kindness . . ." Gernsheim, *Victoria R.*, 154-5.

CHAPTER NINE: A Ruler Alone

p. 99, "We have buried . . ." Thompson, *Queen Victoria*, 50.

p. 99, "I have no rest . . ." Hibbert, *Queen Victoria*, 160.

p. 100, "My pulse gets . . ." Ibid., 165.

p. 100, "scarcely got any . . ." Gernsheim, *Victoria R.*, 140.

p. 100, "For me, life came . . ." Ibid.

p. 100, "*no human power* . . ." Strachey, *Queen Victoria*, 143.

p. 100, "a *real* comfort . . ." Gernsheim, 147.

p. 102, "Now all, all . . ." St. Aubyn, *Queen Victoria*, 423.

p. 103, "a cruelly misunderstood . . ." Strachey, *Queen Victoria*, 342.

p. 103, "the Queen's *sorrows* that . . ." Ibid., 314.

p. 105, "terribly shaken . . ." Gernsheim, *Victoria R.*, 146.

p. 107, "The Lower Classes . . ." Longford, *Queen Victoria*, 352.

p. 107, "mad and utterly . . ." St. Aubyn, *Queen Victoria*, 368.

p. 107, "let women be what . . ." Ibid., 219.

p. 108, "He speaks to . . ." Strachey, *Queen Victoria*, 167.

CHAPTER TEN: Home Rule

p. 112, "the law is openly . . ." Hibbert, *Queen Victoria*, 266.

p. 112, "If there are not sufficient . . ." Ibid., 271.

p. 113, "Ireland stands . . ." Longford, *Queen Victoria*, 491.

p. 114, "The behavior of the . . ." Hibbert, *Queen Victoria*, 302.

p. 114, "I feel very deeply . . ." Ibid., 301.

p. 114, "into the shaking . . ." Gernsheim, *Victoria R.*, 211.

CHAPTER ELEVEN: Conflicts at Home and Abroad

p. 119, "the *extreme iniquity* . . ." Gernsheim, *Victoria R.*, 151.

p. 120, "she [the queen] *cannot...*" Longford, *Queen Victoria,* 443.

p. 121, "the very worst . . ." St. Aubyn, *Queen Victoria,* 416.

p. 122, "I never refuse . . ." Gernsheim, *Victoria R.,* 149.

p. 123, "You have heard . . ." Strachey, *Queen Victoria,* 346.

p. 126, "If the Queen were . . ." Ibid., 177.

p. 126, "I never saw . . ." Hibbert, *Queen Victoria,* 250.

p. 126, "If England is . . ." Strachey, *Queen Victoria,* 363.

p. 127, "peace with honor" Longford, *Queen Victoria,* 115.

p. 128, "The *true economy . . .*" Gernsheim, *Victoria R.,* 157.

p. 128, "We must, with our . . ." Hibbert, *Queen Victoria,* 259.

p. 129, "sooner abdicate than . . ." Ibid., 260.

p. 129, "I am so overdone . . ." Gernsheim, *Victoria R.,* 157.

p. 129, "the queen alone . . ." Ibid.

p. 131, "We must not retire . . ." Hibbert, *Queen Victoria,* 289.

p. 131, "responsible by imprudence . . ." St. Aubyn, *Queen Victoria,* 455.

CHAPTER TWELVE: "I Will Be Good"

p. 136, "All was worthy . . ." St. Aubyn, *Queen Victoria,* 492.

p. 136, "It is impossible for . . ." Hibbert, *Queen Victoria,* 307.

p. 138, "How long will . . ." Thompson, *Queen Victoria,* 119.

p. 139, "All right, thank you . . ." Gernsheim, *Victoria R.,* 161.

p. 139, "When she insists . . ." Thompson, *Queen Victoria,* 122-3.

p. 140, "Today is the day . . ." St. Aubyn, *Queen Victoria,* 545.

p. 140, "From my heart . . ." Gernsheim, *Victoria R.,* 214.

p. 140, "The streets, the windows . . ." St. Aubyn, *Queen Victoria,* 546.

p. 140, "God knows there is . . ." Strachey, *Queen Victoria,* 206.

p. 140, "Another year . . ." St. Aubyn, *Queen Victoria,* 592.

p. 142, "Oh, Albert" Ibid., 596.

p. 145, "mad, wicked folly" Strachey, *Queen Victoria,* 409.

Bibliography

Gernsheim, Helmut, and Alison Gernsheim. *Victoria R.* New York: G. P. Putnam's Sons, 1959.

Grant, Neil. *Victoria: Queen and Empress.* New York: Franklin Watts, Inc., 1970.

Hibbert, Christopher, ed. *Queen Victoria in Her Letters and Journals.* New York: Viking, 1985.

Longford, Elizabeth. *Queen Victoria: Born to Succeed.* New York: Harper & Row, Publishers, 1964.

Reader, W. J. *Life in Victorian England.* London: B. T. Batsford Limited, 1964.

Strachey, Lytton. *The Illustrated Queen Victoria.* New York: Weidenfeld & Nicolson, 1987.

———. *Queen Victoria.* New York: Harcourt, Brace & World, Inc., 1921.

St. Aubyn, Giles. *Queen Victoria: A Portrait.* New York: Atheneum, 1992.

Thompson, Dorothy. *Queen Victoria: The Woman, The Monarch, and The People.* New York: Pantheon Books, 1990.

Woodham-Smith, Cecil. *Queen Victoria: From Her Birth to the Death of the Prince Consort.* New York: Alfred A. Knopf, 1972.

Web sites

Assassination Attempts
http://www.users.uniserve.com/~canyon/attempts.html/

Empires: Queen Victoria (PBS)
http://www.pbs.org/empires/victoria/

The Life and Times of Queen Victoria
http://www.victorianstation.com/queen.html

Queen Victoria: a Concise Biography
http://landow.stg.brown.edu/victorian/vn/victor6.html

Index